T0339501

The Sustainable Manifesto

In *The Sustainable Manifesto*, Kersten Reich describes in a concise and memorable way the necessary actions that humans need to take to live sustainably and combat climate change.

Are we sufficiently capable of changing our behavior toward sustainability? What do we have to do in a more sustainable way and how? *The Sustainable Manifesto* considers questions around behavior change and action for sustainability and connects this thinking to current research in both the natural and human sciences. Reich begins by addressing the most important risks to sustainability and looks in particular at climate change, biodiversity, land use, and global phosphorus and nitrogen cycles. He goes on to identify the main causes that have led to the current crisis: Specifically the human desire for expansion, growth in all areas, progress, and competitive advantages that have forced consideration of the common good into the background. In this vein, the author highlights how economics and politics are two driving forces for which sustainability is difficult to comprehend, going against their basic principles of a liberal and now neoliberal expansion of all markets. Finally, Reich demonstrates how sustainability could be possible if we reprioritize our life goals and face the reality of an ecological crisis and the necessary transformation of society in order to save our planet.

Innovative and accessible, this book will be of interest to students and researchers of sustainability, theories of learning, human behavior, as well as those who are looking for answers on how to fight for a sustainable future.

Kersten Reich is a University Professor at the University of Köln and the founder of Interactive Constructivism, a brand of constructivism that is culturally orientated and stands in proximity with pragmatism (especially Deweyan pragmatism). He is codirector of the Dewey-Center at the University of Cologne. He is the author of over 120 papers and 30 books, including some on Dewey, Interactive Constructivism, and more recently on sustainability.

Routledge Focus on Environment and Sustainability

Natural Resource Leadership and Management
A Practical Guide for Professionals
Frederick Cubbage

Monetary Policy and Food Inflation in Emerging and Developing Economies
Abdul-Aziz Iddrisu and Imhotep Paul Alagidede

Mathematical Models and Environmental Change
Case Studies in Long Term Management
Douglas J. Crookes

German Radioactive Waste
Changes in Policy and Law
Robert Rybski

The Sustainable Manifesto
A Commitment to Individual, Economical, and Political Change
Kersten Reich

Phyto and Microbial Remediation of Heavy Metals and Radionuclides in the Environment
An Eco-Friendly Solution for Detoxifying Soils
Salah-Tazdaït and Djaber Tazdaït

Water Governance in Bolivia
Cochabamba since the Water War
Nasya Sara Razavi

For more information about this series, please visit: www.routledge.com/ Routledge-Focus-on-Environment-and-Sustainability/book-series/ RFES

The Sustainable Manifesto

A Commitment to Individual, Economical, and Political Change

Kersten Reich

LONDON AND NEW YORK

from Routledge

First published 2022
by Routledge
4 Park Square, Milton Park, Abingdon, Oxon OX14 4RN

and by Routledge
605 Third Avenue, New York, NY 10158

Routledge is an imprint of the Taylor & Francis Group, an informa business

British Library Cataloguing-in-Publication Data
A catalogue record for this book is available from the British Library

Library of Congress Cataloging-in-Publication Data
A catalog record has been requested for this book

ISBN: 978-1-032-23250-8 (hbk)
ISBN: 978-1-032-23249-2 (pbk)
ISBN: 978-1-003-27644-9 (ebk)

DOI: 10.4324/9781003276449

Typeset in Times New Roman
by SPi Technologies India Pvt Ltd (Straive)

Contents

Preface

A sustainable movement is challenging the world – a movement that seeks to stand in the way of an approaching crisis, a catastrophe that threatens the survival of all people and all life on earth. Today, this movement is no longer an awakening proletariat and class struggle, but a movement for sustainability that confronts the general endangerment of our living conditions. What are the opponents? All the powers of the economy, which are only interested in profit maximization and for which business as usual is more useful than to bear the costs and necessities of a radical ecological transformation. All forces of politics that have allied themselves with an economy of constant growth and pay homage to a constituency of consumption. All consumers who put self-interest and satisfaction before their impact on nature and the environment. All these forces have consciously or unconsciously allied themselves to chase away the sustainable movement through denial, omission, and reinterpretation.

The Sustainable Manifesto is a political statement about the state of affairs; about what people would have to do in order to still save their world but so far are not willing to do. But if we don't start to act immediately and face reality, our planet will be unsalvageable, and humans who roam in abundance will have overstepped the boundaries of the earth too many times. Where is the opposition that does not only meet on Fridays in front of schools, that does not only complain about climate change at conferences, that does not only constantly lead new debates about what has to be done for more sustainability? Where is the opposition that clearly takes responsibility and names the damaging polluters? Where is the resistance of the sustainable movement who has understood that scientific research can clearly show the consequences of climate change, the extinction of species, the effects of resource depletion on the future, the degradation of our air and water, and the unfairness of the distribution of costs and burdens of a lack of sustainability?

Where are the sustainable ones who know that it is precisely in the probabilities that the sciences can calculate and present that there is the possibility for a new policy of "truth," that they can oppose stupidity and shortsightedness and the greed of profit for ruthless gains for all our future survival? How can this knowledge become a force of change?

The Sustainable Manifesto reflects my extensive research as a learning researcher and cultural theorist who has studied human behavior in a broad and holistic way for more than 50 years, seeking to answer the question of why people are still too hesitant to intervene together immediately, even when disaster is clearly in front of them. We often imagine our learning as successful in any way; has it now failed us? On the one hand, this manifesto probably comes too soon because most people are too little prepared to take truly radical steps toward greater sustainability. All measures imply fundamental changes in behavior, mostly renunciation, and such changeover always seems to come too soon. Moreover, it is currently difficult to imagine nations agreeing comprehensively on a common sustainability by a majority rather than always announcing a new agenda that is then only half-heartedly pursued because such decisions could cost votes. Fundamentally, it is hard to imagine all of humanity quickly agreeing and committing – because it never has. This manifesto comes too late in other respects because many of the earth's boundaries have already been crossed and majorities are not yet arguing for a radical change.

Let's hope; it may already be late, but not too late: Sustainable people of this world, unite, let us save the planet together!

Structure of the Manifesto

The manifesto will proceed in three steps:

First, important facts of the crisis will be summarized to make the situation clear.

In a second part, the origins of today's patterns of thinking and acting are discussed: Our behavior comes from old times, which often led to success in the past, but no longer fits the circumstances today. A look at human history can help to make things clear: We live in a new time and must learn to think anew!

In the third and most comprehensive part, consequences are to be drawn: What do we have to do? How can our planet still be saved?

1 Starting Point: What Are the Facts of the Crisis?

In the history of all previous societies, sustainability was primarily intended to serve economic, social, political, and cultural purposes and to be carried on from generation to generation. Humanity was successful in this sense of its very own sustainability: It exploited natural resources, produced greenhouse gases, and gradually imposed its lifestyle on the entire world. Today, the refusal to sufficiently take responsibility for one's own legacy on the planet brings humanity to the limits of its existence, endangers the planet, and deprives people of the possibility of leaving a world to children that offers chances for life as before.

What Are the Major Facts and Challenges?

For thousands of years, humans had little influence on natural events. They were at their mercy but triggered them themselves only to a small extent through their actions. We can still see traces of humanity in many places, for example in the great pyramids that have been left to us as symbols of human activities, which, however, were not harmful to the course of the world on planet Earth. People have always had to bear the consequences of activities: Achieve success or suffer defeat. The further we advance to the present time, the more legacies, ruins, and monuments from the past we see, but the real attack on the planet occurred only in the age of industrialization and further expansion since the age of the world wars. The pinnacle of this, so far, has been the atomic bombs, which can destroy all life over a wide area and damage it for a long time.

Damage against living beings and the planet can have many external causes, but here the term "sustainability" focuses on self-made, human causation.[1] Let us imagine that we humans are locusts. We raid all possible food sources and eat everything that comes our way. We

DOI: 10.4324/9781003276449-1

instinctively do what guarantees our survival and at the same time drives us to our own demise because when everything is eaten up, there is nothing left for us either. Nature compensates for such damage in evolution in such a way that the locusts have predators. This limits them. Alone we are not locusts; humans have no greater predators on Earth than themselves. This means humans need to think about the sustainability of their actions when they become so destructive that they wipe out countless species, change the climate, raise sea levels, and trigger many effects that make survival on the planet difficult, even for humans. For in their shortsightedness, humans are depriving themselves of their own livelihoods and future.

As early as 1962, Rachel Carson[2] launched an environmental movement with her book *Silent Spring*. She was reacting to the fact that humans were initiating the death of birds and other creatures through the intensive use of pesticides, which seemed programmatic of the ruthlessness of our treatment of nature. Since then, conditions have continued to worsen, and the wake-up call has reached humanity only to a limited extent. Today we speak of the Anthropocene.[3] By this, scientific research aims to capture a new geochronological epoch in which humans have become the most important factor influencing geological, biological, and atmospheric processes on Earth. It puts humanity itself at risk because humanity, through its actions, transcends the boundaries of the Earth in too many aspects.

The concept of sustainability, first coined by Carl von Carlowitz at the beginning of the 18th century to show that in forestry no more trees should be cut down than will grow back, has today gained a global dimension. But it was not until the publication of the famous study by the Club of Rome in 1972 that sustainability in today's sense came to the attention of the general public,[4] although there were already sufficient signals of the effects of social and, above all, economic developments on the biosphere before then. One need only mention besides the atomic bomb tests, oil damage caused by tanker accidents, soil and climate damage caused by deforestation, the use of pesticides, the heavy consumption of resources that will no longer be available to future generations, and many others.

Since then, the term "sustainability" has focused attention on the fact that in a world of increasing consumption with an enormously increased world population, a balance must be found between all the developments that people initiate and pursue and the effects that these have on the environment and for the future.[5] It is a world of growth with increasing prosperity, an increase in consumer goods, and an abundance that is appreciated as prosperity but feared for ecology.[6]

The criterion for a good balance is the assumption that sustainability can be measured by the extent to which the global needs of the present will still allow future generations to be able to live out their own needs according to high qualitative and social standards. Or to put it in a nutshell: Do we enable future generations to live a life that would also meet our standards in the quality of living, or do we leave them a damaged, difficult, so limited habitable world that they must despise and hate us for it?[7]

The great acceleration of global change triggered by socioeconomic trends are very comprehensively summarized by Steffen et al.[8] These trends, compiled from different databases, show very vividly that (1) population density has grown globally, (2) gross domestic product has increased especially in rich countries, (3) global foreign direct investment has been accumulated, (4) global urban population has increased, (5) global primary energy consumption has led to a hunger for fossil energies, (6) fertilizers are used more and more, (7) large dams are being expanded, (8) water consumption is increasing, (9) paper production is growing, (10) the number of motor vehicles has climate effects, (11) communications connections (Internet and mobile telephony) are expanded, (12) in tourism, the number of trips, measured in arrivals, is increasing.

But this is by no means all the data. In addition, there is the growing amount of garbage, the contamination of the oceans with plastic and pollution of the water, and the extinction of species. Overall, greenhouse gas levels continue to rise,[9] stratospheric ozone is increasing, Earth's surface temperature is rising, ocean acidification is growing, rainforests are dwindling, and many resources are being irrevocably plundered.[10] Let's have a closer look.

In 1972, the Club of Rome presented a forecast on the development of sustainability, which has essentially been confirmed over time.[11] The model calculations have been fulfilled since 1972: A rising population growth, a higher industrial production per capita, a rising prosperity but also a growing pollution, sealing, and poisoning of the world; decreasing reserves of nonrenewable raw materials; and growing food production. Humanity is at the threshold of a dramatic change, which is a sustainable challenge significantly more than climate change. In particular, the decline of nonrenewable resources will have an impact on services per capita and industrial output. The declining curves in population increase, global pollution, and food production are then consequences of a decline that is not due to human renunciation out of insight into climate change but is forced upon humans primarily by their insufficiently sustainable lifestyles.

From about 2030, crisis effects will occur because industrial production will lack raw materials, supply chains cannot be adequately served, droughts and floods will endanger food and human lives, and migration movements will inevitably lead to conflicts if not wars. Especially in the case of climate targets, which are supposed to prevent warming and thus severe ecological consequences for humanity, there is a gap between what actually limits greenhouse gases (implementation gap) but also between the politically necessary targets and the actual political goals that are communicated to the population (ambition gap).

The Club of Rome was an association of experts from more than 30 countries at the time. The conclusion of the study "Limits to Growth" was the following: "If the present increase in world population, industrialization, pollution, food production and exploitation of natural resources continues unabated, the absolute limits to growth on earth will be reached in the course of the next hundred years."[12] The book was torn apart in criticism from both the right and the left because it had not adequately incorporated the dimensions of positive growth for improving social conditions and had been produced by a supposedly dubious elitist circle. Developing countries also complained that the "ecological scarcity discourse" prevented them from adequately participating in the world's wealth in the future. Thus, the most important defenses to date have been named early on. No matter what scientific standards are met to describe climate change more accurately, opponents cling to their wishful images of a world in growth and their dream of not wanting to do without economic development at all costs.

Today, Johann Rockström et al. take a very plausible approach when they speak of planetary boundaries instead of ever-new possibilities (see Stockholm Resilience Centre).[13] In this view, humanity has already exceeded the range of safe limits that can still be managed in four areas: That of (1) climate change, (2) biodiversity, (3) land use, and (4) global phosphorus and nitrogen cycles. In this modeling, rather than describing simple linear trends, the exponential unfolding of change is used. The boundaries are determined by tipping points, the crossing of which is irreversible, expressing that the events that then follow can no longer be controlled by old means.

For planetary boundaries, Steffen et al. have produced a good pictorial representation of the rapid changes that lead to tipping points.[14] They describe a major acceleration of risk factors. As a deceleration of risks, different countries and organizations try to bring order into the tangle of countermeasures by means of standards, seals, ratings, and rankings, which, however, so far expresses rather self-commitments on a hesitant path of change toward more sustainability in rough commitments than a radical change in thinking and acting. The high media presence of the topic seems to express a capacity of humanity to act, but the real implementations show that in the end, it is so far insufficient lip service.

If we summarize the facts about the crisis of sustainability, the following aspects are particularly critical. I will discuss them in six important dimensions.

Population Growth

Simultaneously, with changes in production, in agricultural economy, in the spread of transport, with the increase of better living conditions and higher mobility, an increase in population began in the 18th and 19th centuries. Observant people feared overpopulation at that time. From today's point of view, the fear at that time seems to be unfounded because – even if mortality was very high in earlier times – it did not lead to mass deaths because of productive forms of the agricultural economy. In 1804, there were one billion humans on Earth, and then in 1927, there were two billion. Compared to the beginning, we see an increasing curve. In 2019, the world population was 7.75 billion, the tendency in this century points to 11 billion.

But population density must always be seen in relation to food and other resources, especially with regard to social, humane conditions, in order to adequately provide for the growing mass of people. Today, the problem of growing populations is closely linked to overcoming hunger and misery, increasing social justice, better health, and security, especially in young and old age. The more successfully the challenges are mastered, however, the more problems of sustainability grow. According to Bello, overpopulation creates enormous problems for a sustainable way of life, but people in rich countries, in particular, shy away from addressing this because it could easily be interpreted as politically incorrect if national or even global birth control were introduced.[15]

Economic growth seems to tolerate population growth better than expected, at least in the richer countries, and since the last third of the 20th century, there has even been a countermovement, the more prosperity, the fewer children. In recent decades, humanity has become less concerned about the extent to which the mass of people can be adequately fed, although it has to be emphasized that one-seventh of humanity has to live at subsistence level, and there is always the risk that these people won't survive. Hunger and poverty have accompanied mankind for a long time. With the affluent societies, however, they seemed surmountable because they had decreased significantly in recent decades. Since 2015, however, the number of hungry people has been rising again. In the joint report "The State of Food Security," United Nations (UN) organizations point out that in 2019, over 821 million people still suffered from hunger and had to fight for survival every day.[16] Hunger is extreme in Africa, particularly in East Africa, where more than 30 percent of the population is affected. But other regions of the world, such as the Caribbean, Latin America, and Asia, also experience malnutrition and severe food insecurity, affecting more than two billion people. The UN goal of eliminating hunger by 2030 is becoming a distant prospect in view of the current figures: If climate changes increase, major famines cannot be avoided because drought and desiccation alternate regionally with floods and crop failures worldwide. This will lead to overall losses that could only be compensated for if the rich countries voluntarily gave away much more of their wealth.

Population growth proves to be a constant challenge, especially in terms of hunger, water supply, and poverty of many people. Population density affects the planet as a whole, leading to more exploitation of the world's resources, more consumption, more industries that pollute the environment, and more and more waste at the end of a chain of production and consumption. Young people expect to be able to maintain at least the same lifestyles and standards of living as their parents.

The growth of garbage dumps, the world enriched with fine dust, the traffic collapse because of more and more flights, ships, cars, and trucks, more and more compacted traffic areas; the oceans flooded with plastic are symptoms of an ecological crisis that grows with an increasing population and simultaneously increasing consumer desires. Transport of goods as well as travel and tourism are part of the standard of living of the present, but ecologically, they are consistently harmful in mass form as an expression of the increase in consumption, the feeling of freedom, and the longing for space.

In addition, it must be taken into account that the increase in population in many countries significantly forces the consumption of natural resources and strengthens the pollution, which would become even worse if living standards were improved worldwide. However, should poverty and hunger decrease against the previous trajectory, as the UN calls for in the global goals, this also creates the problem of growing resource consumption and the increase in meat consumption, water consumption, and the release of further greenhouse gases, to name just a few elementary factors. Thus, the humane goal of reducing hunger and misery leads in equal measure to an aggravation of the ecological crisis, as long as low-polluting forms of production cannot be offered at a low cost. This is a paradox in the UN's global goals that currently seems almost impossible to resolve.

Humanity encounters opposing trends. Where some go hungry, others are overfed and have the opposite problem of overweight and obesity – this trend is also on the rise. It shows not only an unequal distribution of wealth and abundance but also that wealth alone does not make people act sustainably. In 2018, about four million people died from obesity. This group of people in particular, because they consume significantly more and especially meat, is at the same time responsible for particularly negative values in the ecological balance sheet.

Population growth is linked to all areas, which is why simple targets on specific areas, such as hunger, poverty, and water, in particular, are unfortunately usually too simplistic in their thinking because they do not adequately capture the inner interconnectedness and dynamics of factors. Humanity is specialized to research and observe in delimited segments, the complex and dynamically linked effects are often overlooked in simplified models. The global challenge of population density is therefore in tension with all the following factors because every increase in the number of people simultaneously creates a new footprint.

Climate Change

The increase in greenhouse gases is leading to climate change, the consequences of which are becoming more and more clear: An increased average temperature with extremes of temperature and weather, ice melting, rising sea levels. But just as the climate is more than the current weather, the sustainability crisis is also more than the climate crisis, which is the focus of rich countries today.

The limits to growth predicted by the Club of Rome have arrived. Media coverage and translation into many languages have made people aware that there is a lack of sustainability. Problem noticed, but how urgent is it really?

In the example of the lily pond that has become famous, the Club of Rome report also already mentioned the problem of tipping points, which is repeatedly cited today for climate change. "Suppose you own a pond on which a water lily grows. The lily plant doubles in size every day. If the lily were allowed to grow unhindered, it would completely cover the pond in 30 days, suffocating the other forms of life in the water. For a long time, the lily plant seems small, and until it covers half the pond, you decide not to worry and don't cut it back. On what day will it cover half the pond? On the twenty-ninth day, of course. You have one day to save your pond."[17]

Even if some results of the 1972 study can be described more precisely today, even if many new areas have been added, the tendency of the statement has been confirmed and intensified. If we continue as before, if emerging countries enter into the same consumption as the richer ones, then the 30th day will be reached long before 2100, which was the assumption a few years ago. It is true that industry and politics, in particular, clinging to the old, unchecked ideas of growth, claim that above all scientific-technological development and the decline in population growth – not yet in absolute figures, but at least in a lower growth rate – mean that the last day of comprehensive capacity to act can still be postponed, but basically everyone who informs themselves scientifically knows that humanity must already deal more sustainably with the earth today. However, many people console themselves with the fact that it does not seem to be possible to determine exactly what comprehensive capacity to act means on the last day. After the crisis seems to be before the crisis. And even if there are tipping points, not everything will go under. But is our knowledge sufficient to assert this?

Human-made climate change is even fundamentally denied by some people. The main argument is that climate fluctuations have always existed. That is true. But the deduction that it is a matter of purely natural fluctuations is simply wrong. Neukom and others (2019) write in *Nature* that scientifically there is a significant difference between earlier cold and warm periods and the current warming.[18] In the past, the changes were more regional and they occurred at different times. Today, they are global, and they occur simultaneously. Their study, which covers the land and the sea, analyzed climate data from the international research group Past Global Changes. Sources of these studies include tree growth rings, ice cores and lake sediments, changes in corals, and more, in addition to existing measured data. All the studies agree: The greenhouse gas carbon dioxide (CO_2) has been identified as the main cause of global warming. It can be absorbed from the atmosphere by vegetation, there are several cycles of how it can be created and processed without increasing exponentially. But the current warming shows that the regenerative cycle has been interrupted by humanity through the increase of greenhouse gases. The biosphere with the emitted CO_2 gases becomes a greenhouse that drives global warming, which triggers another chain of events such as ice melting, thawing of permafrost, rising sea levels, and extreme weather and climate phenomena.[19] This effect is having a greater impact day by day. Since the beginning of the industrial revolution, we have been dealing with a continuous and increasingly powerful warming, which is taking place at an ever-faster and continuously increasing rate.

The most important greenhouse gas is CO_2. Human-made CO_2 is mainly produced by burning fossil fuels. Meat consumption also contributes significantly to greenhouse gases because of its mass production methods.[20] The ecological footprint calculates against this production how much forest would be needed to offset CO_2 and presents this in areas. The existing forest, and even more a forest that could be cultivated, could then bind the CO_2 as biomass, as a living plant, or as humus to prevent the greenhouse effect. This calculation is also rather glossed over instead of viewed as critically complex. This is because the oceans are also assumed to store CO_2, even though ocean acidification by CO_2 represents its own planetary boundary. In 2017, CO_2 concentrations were 41 percent above preindustrial levels. Ocean acidification is reflected in the pH of the sea surface, which is falling as CO_2 is trapped. It has become so poor that many marine species are threatened by it, especially because calcium carbonate cannot attach well at lower pH levels. Many effects contribute to the decline of the ocean as a CO_2 reservoir. First, it is the warming of the oceans that has an unfavorable effect. But also the overfishing and pollution of the oceans by the fishing industry worsen the situation because the fish in the sea make an essential contribution to an ecological balance. In addition, the fishing industry produces a lot of plastic in the sea because it feeds its nets and other pollutants in an uncontrolled way.[21]

The climate targets, given in degrees and goals that are still "allowed," are based on scientific analysis, but they are set arbitrarily by politicians. No one can say whether 1 degree, 1.5 degrees, or 2 degrees are sufficient limits to actually implement climate change in a "compatible" way (for whom, for which places, in which range) in a long-time perspective. To simplify the complicated scientific penetration, currently, the two-degree target has more or less become politically accepted. This assumes the probability that the climate changes, which will then occur, will already be severe, but will not endanger humanity as a whole.

Scientific models work with probabilities; they cannot predict absolutely which individual events will occur and exactly when. And the dangers generated by climate change, until they are felt by all people in all regions, may initially vary widely. Some countries will be more affected than others by rising sea levels, flooding or prolonged drought, and major wildfires. Many countries in the global south are particularly at risk from floods, storms, and droughts. Rising sea levels threaten coasts and islands in the tropics in particular; according to the World Risk Index, countries such as Vanuatu, Tonga, Dominica, the Solomon Islands, and Fiji will be the first to be affected.[22]

Temperatures in densely populated areas will rise more than over the oceans; currently, the changes are most pronounced in the Arctic. What the thawing of the permafrost will mean is still a matter of debate, even among scientists. Extreme weather events, as the present already shows, will increase sharply. Heavy precipitation with flooding on the one hand, and periods of drought with increasing fire danger on the other, are two expressions of a changing climate.[23]

Risks are on the rise with warming for human food and water supplies, which is important for the survival and health of many people. Corn, wheat, and rice will be at risk in terms of yields, particularly in Africa, Southeast Asia, and South America. According to model calculations, water supplies can no longer be guaranteed in some countries at 1.5 degrees and are twice as critical at 2 degrees Celsius. Even if climate warming is considered moderate by politicians, the health risks that already exist in certain countries, especially in the global south, will increase.

What is often forgotten are the consequences of climate change on the earth's building fabric. Roads, bridges, buildings, and all other constructs are subject to severe deterioration, especially due to extreme weather events.[24] The budget coffers of the countries are usually too little for such renewal and already show a tendency to let the existing substance decay in many cases.

Optimists among scientists, and even more so in business and politics, like to focus on technologies to contain climate gases and reduce them from the atmosphere through geoengineering. For example, by inoculating the stratosphere with sulfur dioxide, the stratosphere could reflect solar radiation back into space via aerosols to reduce the greenhouse effect; nanoparticles could also be used for this purpose. Critics of this optimism point out that this would create further unpredictable climate effects that could lead to further catastrophic scenarios.[25] Quite apart from this, there is simply not enough time to develop such technologies comprehensively in sufficient quantities and to deploy them quickly. This also applies to the generation of negative emissions by capturing and storing CO_2 from the atmosphere. It would be simpler if CO_2-consuming forests and plants (biomass) were immediately grown en masse to reduce CO_2. The limitation here is private ownership of land and agricultural land, scarce nutrients, and availability of water. In addition, the time effect required to grow such biomass cannot be neglected. Even if the planning of such measures works with long-term effects, they would probably be the most realistic measures of CO_2 reduction in the near future. But at the moment, humanity is still engaged in containing further slash and burn of existing forests, and not even with great success. The bigger problem, however, is that even with effective climate mitigation measures that include CO_2 reductions, further increasing economic growth will quickly counteract such effects.[26]

There are now a great many compilations of further climate facts. For a list of facts, which are summarized here, see climate G20.[27] Key points are as follows:

Air temperature: The average global air temperature is currently one degree higher than the 20th-century average; in some countries, the two-degree path is already on its way. There are always new record years of annual average and maximum temperatures in the last ten years. The mean air temperature has been steadily rising. Each decade is warmer than the previous one. The decade 2011 to 2020 forms a new record high. Temperature records are an expression of this.[28]

Ice melt: Glaciers and snow are diminishing; in particular, the Greenland ice sheet is melting by 250 to 300 billion tons per year. The sea ice around the North and South Poles is also diminishing. Four-fifths of mountain glaciers are currently losing large ice masses. The rate of ice loss is accelerating.

Floods and severe weather events: Major weather events with flooding are increasing. Over the past 30 years, such events have increased two- to threefold. Insurers of such losses also report a tripling of losses from thunderstorms. Climate events last longer and weather patterns do not change as quickly as they used to. This amplifies weather effects.

Heat and drought: Human existence depends on an ambient temperature that is cooler than body temperature, thus exerting a cooling effect on the body. Although occasional sweating may be pleasant, humans require a cooling environment on a permanent basis. The uniqueness of planet Earth in the cosmos, as we know it, is its climate, which is conducive to life. Since we are talking about average temperatures, just a few degrees more are enough to have far-reaching consequences. A few degrees are already sufficient to generate regionally dangerous heat, to let drought grow in certain regions, and to increase bush fires. What is particularly tragic here is that human greed contributes negatively to the effects. The burning of large parts of the Amazon rainforest is at the forefront of a behavior that not only directly releases greenhouse gases but also permanently destroys large CO_2 reservoirs. World politics has not formed sufficient sanctions for this, although the action threatens humanity as a whole. And, for example, Australia's government, which suffered the largest bushfires of modern times in 2019–2020, is only hesitantly moving away from climate denial toward policies that believe the catastrophe is linked to climate change. Even catastrophic events aren't enough to make the case for rejecting the fossil fuel economy.

Changes in agriculture and forestry: Warming temperatures are changing flowering and harvesting times. Compared with the 1970s, apple trees in many countries are blossoming around 20 days earlier, although it is then easier for frost damage to occur at night and for harvests to fail later. Numerous tree species are at risk because they are slow to adapt to climate changes. Dry summers with an increased risk of forest fires or heavy precipitation with flooding threaten the population. At the same time, insects are migrating that have no predators; on the other hand, there is a lack of insects for pollination. The changes are burdening agriculture and forestry. Even an ecological oriented agriculture is confronted with complicated questions of economic efficiency due to climate change because consumers always want to save money. Food production and a possible increase in population as a result of this have numerous consequential effects, leading in particular to an expansion of production areas, a reduction in the types of cultivation with a destruction of species and plant diversity in order to specifically satisfy the mass needs of people. More than 75 percent of food today comes from 12 plant species and 5 animal species.[29] The destruction of ecologically significant rainforests dramatically demonstrate how ecologically valuable and irrecoverable biotopes are being destroyed for animal feed. Herbicides, pesticides, and antibiotics are unleashed on the ecology to maximize costs and benefits, irretrievably interfering with nature's cycles. This happens because, throughout history, human concern has been increasingly focused on maximizing profits and increasing prosperity, ignoring the sustainability traps created in the process. For example, if scientific progress has produced antibiotics as a boon to humanity in the fight against disease, humans are risking this boon by driving it into resistance in factory farming for short profit purposes, turning the boon into a curse. While there are many people who are concerned about this – like vegetarians and vegans – in the mass of production and lifestyle, the concern so far is not enough to escape the traps and effectively eliminate them.

Resource Scarcity

Massive resource extraction of nonregenerative raw materials will soon lead to limitations in industrial production that can no longer be compensated for by inventions and extreme extraction methods alone. Raw materials will become scarce and expensive. The mass cultivation of monocultures and the degradation of soils will lead to overfertilization, deterioration of soil quality, and overall to an overload of the earth. Scientific forecasts say very clearly that in the 21st century, therefore, the population will decrease and the hunger and impoverishment of many people will increase. Conflicts and wars are likely to occur more frequently.

There are many renewable resources in the biosphere, and so a primary goal of sustainable management is to use them while protecting their potency. This goal generates higher costs than a use that is not concerned with preserving the quality of the resources but only serves short-term profits. Consumers are also part of this struggle, which today is fought especially between organic food and cheap food. Even if natural reproduction and evolution offer an almost infinite reservoir of biological renewal, renewable resources can also degrade, lose quality, become overfertilized and negatively determine the phosphorus cycle, they can become enriched with pollutants and leave behind depleted soils or deforested zones.

The situation is bad for nonrenewable resources. They are currently being consumed en masse without regard for future generations. Well-known organic resources are fossil fuels like coal, oil, or gas, which have been consumed since industrialization and led to the greenhouse effect. But there are, meanwhile, long lists of minerals and substances of all kinds, which regenerate only in very long periods, if at all. What is consumed today is no longer available later.

The global feeding of billions of people is currently managed with an agricultural industry that is itself not without problems for sustainability. A basic paradox of capitalist production is that 70 percent of the world's hungry people live where food is produced. Despite overproduction, it has not yet been possible to free these people from hunger. Instead, they serve predominantly as cheap labor to increase the profits of a few people. Increasing mechanization, the use of fertilizers and pesticides, including genetically manipulated seeds, are intended to help further improve yields. Long-lasting soil fertility, water purity, and the preservation of biodiversity thus fall by the wayside. If we look at the world's grain production, more than half is fed to animals, and increasingly processed into fuel, with profit maximization always in the foreground. A lot is wasted because of overproduction. Profits are made with seeds but often at the expense of regionally suitable products since the products offered are not designed for local conditions (soils, pests), forcing further costs for fertilizers and protective measures. This results in dependencies that are extensively served by the agricultural industry as a profit strategy.

The industrialized countries consume significantly more per capita than the poorer countries. While the richer countries primarily share in the value creation from global raw materials, the less developed countries have to bear disproportionately the ecological and social effects of raw material extraction, regional shortages, and expensive prices. Much of the overproduction in rich countries flows back to poor regions of the world to be marketed at low prices. This destroys the local markets, which cannot compete with it. From the abundance of the rich comes the hunger of the poor. This is the capitalist logic: You have to sell something in order to be able to buy something yourself. If an outside supplier enters who produces cheaper than you, this undermines every economy and regional sustainability.

Agricultural production is always directly interconnected with nature and has consequences for biodiversity, climate, conservation, or destruction of natural resources. At the same time, there is a neoliberal market in capitalism, which is not regulated by principles of reason but by principles of profit. For rich countries, it has become clear that they would not only have to reduce production volumes but also make payment in agriculture fairer and regulate overall for more sustainability. This will raise prices. At the same time, consumers would have to adapt to sustainable consumption of more regional food, organic farming, and less meat consumption[30] to support such a development from the demand side. The neoliberal path of constant growth promotion inevitably leads agribusiness into overproduction and then into subsidies and a world market orientation that does more harm than good to the global world. Along the way, it generates high nitrate pollution and other damage, especially from pesticides, and an additional acceleration of species extinction as a result; it also endangers human health.

Natural resources are material as well as energetic and spatial resources of the human standard of living. Consumption of such resources always has consequences for the environment and places a burden on it. In particular, the consumption of nonregenerative resources is associated with harmful interventions in the natural and water balance, is usually energy-intensive, and leads to pollutants in the air, water, and soil.

Every production has a life-cycle assessment, even renewable energies or so-called e-mobility are not free of this. Small or large production volumes make a significant difference. If, for example, there is a mass switch from diesel or gasoline engines to electric cars, then the consequences of resource consumption for batteries and their disposal will become new risk factors for soils, energy production, water pollution, and resource destruction of certain rare raw materials that are hardly calculable in size today. The car industry only wants to sell; it does not care about sustainability. Just as they already used cheating software to make the diesel look good, this will continue with the electric car. The eco-balance of the e-car may be more favorable for the air, but there are still no sufficiently sustainable solutions for the consumption of resources and the waste generated.

Water pollution and soil degradation are gradual processes that occur over time. Both industrial and agricultural production contributes to this, as do private households. It is the sum of all human actions that cause the melting of the ice, the thawing of the permafrost, the increase in greenhouse gases, and other events that are almost never immediately noticeable but in the long-term create or have already created tipping points that will irreversibly change the future.

Particularly important as a means of counteracting all these processes is the preservation of a diverse nature. The Amazon rainforest stands as a symbol for this, which can be used to study how human greed interacts with globalized markets. There appears to be a powerlessness in the UN, which deplores forest dieback but seems to be unable to do anything about it. In order to achieve positive effects, humanity would have to start a huge reforestation program because this alone could achieve regeneration with effective CO_2 reduction.

The human way of life has not only transformed nature into agriculture and thus sealed areas but also development for housing, production, consumption, and traffic has produced an increasing soil sealing. Worldwide, the areas that are not yet sealed are continuously shrinking. Megacities are particularly affected by sealing; traffic areas, in particular, take up a high proportion of sealed land. So not only are raw materials becoming scarce but also the available areas are shrinking. In any case, much land is privately owned, and the earth is already comprehensively distributed.[31]

Oceans and Fresh Water

Sea level has already risen by 19 centimeters in the last 100 years. This is due to melting mountain glaciers and the thermal expansion of warming seawater. Between 1993 and 2017, a mean rise of 0.85 centimeters occurred, but it should be noted that regional differences are very large.

Levermann et al. warn that this increase could multiply.[32] Various studies consider the large bound ice areas in the Arctic and especially the Antarctic as decisive factors in this context. The longer global warming continues, the more dramatic the effects will become. The research group from the Potsdam Institute for Climate Impact Research has calculated a large range of variation depending on greenhouse gas emissions.[33] The increase would be substantial compared to the last 100 years and threatening to coastal regions. If all factors are taken into account – i.e., the expansion of the oceans because of warming, the melting of the Greenland ice sheet, the high mountain glaciers, and the Antarctic ice sheet   then, according to calculations by the research group, an increase of at least 1.5 meters can be expected by the end of the century if the greenhouse effects continue unabated.

People prefer to think in terms of linear curves because that is the best way to map their ever-increasing prosperity. It is difficult for them to imagine exponential curves when they have to reckon with doubling numbers or tipping effects – as in a pandemic or in relation to climate change, for example. Human perception and hazard assessment tend to be short term and myopic in orientation: Long-term thinking and action that transcends generations have always been the exception, not the rule, in human history to date. This can be illustrated by an example: Many model calculations illustrate how strongly the constantly increasing CO_2 emissions would have to be slowed down in order to achieve the climate targets set today to curb climate change. Climate scientists give us 8–12 years to leave the path leading to catastrophe in time. If the current rate of increase continues, we can expect scenarios with at least three degrees higher average global temperatures in the next few decades. Currently, we are on a path that argues more for six or eight degrees, which would mean the end of the world as we know it. Already the two-degree target is barely achievable. And if today a limitation to about two degrees is spoken of as a realistic goal, then this means that an increase is added to the already existing temperature, which in many places is already at 1.5 degrees. So two degrees describe a further increase and not a reduction. The current situation is already too much, and to be honest, measures should be taken to strictly limit any further increase. It must also be considered that the decrease of greenhouse gases requires a very long period of time (up to 1,000 years), so even a radical stop only preserves the achieved and already bad condition.

In particular, the effects of Antarctic melt, which can hardly be estimated, make accurate forecasts difficult. In addition, all calculations have further unknowns, because the melting of the tundra and the release of gases can further accelerate the greenhouse effect.

The ecological footprint does not consider freshwater consumption. Water is considered a biologically neutral circulating variable because it appears to be neither produced nor consumed. This also applies to species extinction, which will be characterized in a moment. But water as a life element, which penetrates all of the previous and the following points of view, is connected to them and must be counted also to the planetary boundaries. First of all, the ocean is a gigantic CO_2 reservoir. About 38,000 gigatons of CO_2 (1 gigaton = 1 billion tons) are stored in the oceans. The oceans contain 16 times as much carbon as the terrestrial biosphere – that is, plants and the underlying soils. However, with rising temperatures – one of the additional pitfalls of global warming – this storage power is diminishing. The excess of CO_2 in the atmosphere causes the pH value of the water to change too. The oceans are acidifying.[34] This makes it, for example, difficult for calcifying organisms to produce their skeletons, and because these organisms form the basis for further food chains, domino effects occur that extend to human food production. When the pH level drops, the consequences are alarming: "Like the Richter scale, the pH scale is logarithmic, so even such a small numerical difference represents a very large real-world change."[35] Coral bleaching and the extinction of many species are evidence of this. And the fishing industry with overfishing and destruction of the seabed by trawls accelerates the decline.[36] What is particularly dramatic is the potency of the change that will unfold its own tipping points in water quality and species extinction. In many marine regions, this has already become obvious and measurable.

Increasing water pollution is a global challenge anyway. Plastic waste leaking from land into the sea has reached tremendous proportions. By 2025, it is estimated that for every three tons of fish in the ocean, there is already one ton of trash; by 2050, there will be more plastic than fish.[37] The nutrient load of waters and oceans is rising worldwide, primarily because of overfertilization. This leads not only to unpleasant effects, such as huge algae carpets, but also to a decline in biodiversity. In addition, clean drinking water is not only unequally distributed around the world but also increasingly difficult to produce, making it more expensive. Industrial production and agricultural production consume vast amounts of water that are withdrawn from other cycles. In water-poor countries, in particular, there is an undersupply of drinking water.

Water and waste form a single unit, as both soluble and insoluble substances, especially plastics, end up in the water cycle. Therefore, the protection of water that is as pure as possible is a high goal with which humanity has been very careless. Drinking water alone is usually paid for, whereas its pollution has so far cost basically nothing.

Waste, Pollutants, Poisoning

When people calculate the ecological footprint today, they usually exclude the waste generated by human actions and productions from the calculations, which express how much area in hectares must be determined to define the footprint. Human effects on the negative footprint don't translate easily into areas. Waste, first of all, is all the biodegradable waste that is considered neutral. But neutral in this sense is then also the huge algae carpets that were created in the sea through overfertilization. Then there is so-called landfillable waste, which is expected to decompose over a longer period of time. This is calculated, but other wastes are usually left out of the determination of the ecological footprint. Finally, we have the actual waste that cannot be biologically absorbed. At the top of this waste are plastic, toxic, and radioactive materials, which form their own footprints that have not yet been included in the ecological footprint. And how should we also measure in detail the ruins and legacies of industrial societies, where they are hidden and concealed as garbage because this garbage makes high costs for the polluters? It is true that there are possibilities to recycle many materials but especially the final disposal of nuclear waste shows that there are not even sufficiently tenable calculations that could state how much waste could be positively offset. As long as missing repositories and reactor accidents dramatically show that the risks are incalculable, all positive offsets seem to be rather fictitious anyway. It is to be observed that humanity develops above all a concern for itself, for its short- to medium-term supply, without sufficiently considering a long-term perspective and the effect on the entire world.[38] This will become especially critical if nuclear energy is to replace fossil fuels as a supposedly clean solution.

Extinction of Species

Kolbert has illustrated extinction vividly for individual species to confront us with the dimension and drama of the event.[39] For example, the five extinctions that preceded the present one in the past 600 million years involved the dinosaurs about 65 million years ago. But after all previous extinctions, which may well have affected up to about 75 percent of all species, evolution continued and gave new species a chance. However, from a human point of view, the time required for such a renewal is infinitely long, and it can only succeed if the environment recovers quickly. The climatic and ecological window that makes life on Earth possible has special conditions: A temperature favorable for survival, sufficient water and evaporation rain cycles, large oceans, a favorable atmosphere with oxygen, and many other conducive living conditions. Such favorable conditions for life are probably extremely rare even in space, at least as far as humans can detect.

In May 2019, the global report of the World Biodiversity Council of the UN organization Intergovernmental Platform on Biodiversity and Ecosystem Services (IPBES) was published.[40] This study shows that more than one million animal and plant species are currently endangered and threatened with extinction. While the other five mass extinctions were most likely caused by volcanic disasters and impacts from cosmic bodies that changed the climate and environmental conditions so rapidly that plant and animal life could not adapt quickly enough, humans are considered solely responsible for the sixth extinction scenario currently underway. The IPBES report summarizes the key reasons for the current extinction. The reasons listed here describe impacts in order of what has already been achieved and the magnitude of the impacts:[41]

- Loss of habitat: Humans have increasingly colonized and occupied all land on Earth;
- Changes in land use: Agribusiness leads to monocultures and destroys the diversity not only of free nature but also of agricultural use;
- Hunting and poaching: Species extinction is accelerated by human interests;
- Climate change: Global warming has numerous consequences for species extinction; it is to be feared that climate change will become a dominant aspect for the accelerated process of extinction;
- Environmental toxins, as well as the appearance of alien and invasive species (neobiota): Human intervention on the one hand destroys the diversity of species and on the other hand promotes the migration of certain species with negative effects for the previous state of evolution.

The trend of the sixth, human-made extinction is clear: Biodiversity – i.e., the diversity of species on Earth – is being so massively affected by humans, as is the diversity of ecosystems. Today, more than one million species are threatened and an estimated 70 to 200 species disappear every day. This is very high even in view of a large number of species – an estimated two million have been discovered – yet species extinction is only just beginning and is accelerating. Here, humans themselves are also affected in their diet because species and gene losses also fundamentally threaten the diversity of cultivated plants and the ecological balance that has evolved over long periods of evolution.[42]

Following the Rio Earth Summit, hundreds of scientists produced the report "Sustaining Life," which highlights how human life depends on other species.[43] This dependency and the services provided by the evolution of various life-forms to humans for their own survival, which also seem to be provided by the wider environment as a matter of course, are ignored and overlooked in human actions because they have become accustomed to focusing only on their material benefits and desires. Against this background, they tend to forget the long-time effects of the planetary boundaries.

On the one hand, the species extinction is closely related to the climate crisis; on the other hand, it is at the same time related to the increase in population density and the environmentally destructive interests of humans. This problem is probably even more difficult to solve than the climate crisis, which after all has a clear goal in the reduction of CO_2 emissions. But how to limit the egoism and possessiveness in the conquest of the planet's surfaces?

Nowadays, there are a variety of different, often regionally specific, reasons for species extinction. The cutting down of the rainforest requires other measures than the conversion of intensive agriculture in the industrialized countries in Europe and the USA. The trade in protected species in Asia is a problem all of its own. The main challenge, however, is that no profits can be made with measures against species extinction, that there are no simple and technical solutions, that people could only strengthen biodiversity with insight and renunciation of previous behavior.

Weapons of Mass Destruction

Weapons of mass destruction, which humans can use in nuclear, biological, or chemical warfare to destroy not only humanity but also virtually all life on the planet, are almost not mentioned in the sustainability agenda. Yet the threat has not diminished since the first atomic bombs were dropped and biological and chemical warfare agents have been used in numerous wars and conflicts; in fact, modernizations of the inventory have made it even greater.

Both the increasing defense budgets of countries and the growing number of nuclear warheads are a striking expression of this. In 2019, the United States and Russia had nearly 12,600 warheads, with about 300 each distributed among China and France, and the smaller remainder among the United Kingdom, Pakistan, India, Israel, and North

Korea. The destructive power of even smaller nuclear arsenals is still monstrous. Significantly, for reasons of secrecy, we know very little about the true arsenals of such weapons of mass destruction but can be sure that they will be sufficient to destroy the planet several times over.

In terms of military spending, the United States is the top spender with $649 billion in 2018, which exceeds the total military spending of China ($250 billion), Russia ($61.4 billion), Saudi Arabia ($67.6 billion), India ($66.5 billion), France ($63.8 billion), the United Kingdom ($50 billion), and Germany ($49.5 billion).[44] It is one of humanity's great feats of suppression that after the end of the Cold War, when the threat still seemed very real to many people, the increased threat posed by the expansion of weapons arsenals was hardly discussed widely and comprehensively. Formerly referred to as NBC (nuclear, biological, and chemical) weapons, these weapons are now being mass-produced more than ever. Especially in the case of biological and chemical weapons, there are unknown threats because of secrecy, which can hardly be calculated. In the future, drone armament will make drone warfare possible, facilitating killings and destruction from afar. Arming drones with NBC-weapons may significantly exacerbate the situation.

Alongside military armament has come civilian equipment, which also must be regarded as dangerous. It is certainly worth considering whether the mass proliferation of firearms worldwide, which kills about half a million people a year, should already be described as a strategy of mass destruction or whether several million people must first die in wars before the conceptual classification appears to be correct.

During the Cold War, there was an arms race between the United States and the Soviet Union; today, the term is hardly used. But this, too, is a displacement performance because even if the states like to speak of a highly technological and at the same time defensive arms race, it is always about the possibility of aggressive warfare, which can turn from the defensive into an offensive. The increase in arms deliveries worldwide, which has been observed for decades, is an essential indicator of how much humanity believes in its own self-destruction. In particular, the deliveries from democratic countries to crisis areas show the hypocrisy of a capitalist system that has turned destruction into a business model, while at the same time talking about the security needs of humanity.

Weapons of mass destruction are, and remain, an immediate threat to the present and the future because they can be used at any time, especially since, apart from mutual deterrence, there is no hope that they will not be used in conflict situations. Therefore, peace and a comprehensive peace policy are necessary to protect the future of humanity. However, the greater the rational loss of control by megalomaniac rulers and the more populist arrogance in individual countries grows, the more dangerous the arsenals whose disarmament has remained more wish than reality become.

And the suppression of the threat of mass destruction in the media and the everyday understanding has in turn become a challenge, too. Because awareness of this threat has diminished, fears and concerns about the danger have also weakened. Thus, caution against hasty action may be waning among those who sit at the levers of destruction.

When talking about sustainability for future generations, weapons of mass destruction should not be excluded as a threat. In fact, they are becoming more likely a threat because shortages and ecological disasters will increase, not decrease, the potential for conflicts and wars in the world.

The Negative Footprint

At present, climate change in particular is at the forefront of many considerations. This is quite justified, as climate change fundamentally affects many other factors. Nevertheless, there are a number of additional aspects that have to be considered for the negative footprint. With all aspects discussed so far, it becomes visible that they can never be considered in isolation but are always interrelated. All people need an overview of essential aspects of the situation.

By living on Earth, humans leave a negative footprint that encompasses the biological area and all the life support factors that each person impacts through their lifestyle and standard of living. Such a footprint may appear neutral if it can make the present standard of living equally possible for future generations, but it is negative if it restricts people more in the future than in the present, creates worse living conditions for them, robs them of resources, or negatively alters climate, water, soil, biodiversity. This is a trend that humanity has been increasing heavily since the early 1970s.

The core of a negative footprint is made up of the ecological footprint because the constructors of the theory of the footprint were guided by the question, What biological capacity of the earth is claimed by human activity? In the approach, the average land and water areas available to humans as biocapacity are put in relation to the effects of production. The ecological footprint is fixated on calculating, in particular, the greenhouse gases that are produced to counterbalance them with the biomass that would be needed to provide compensation. It should be noted that in this way, the calculation of arable and pasture land includes both marine areas used for fishing and inland water areas, as well as forests, but not the already existing or built structures or natural areas like deserts and mountains. An illustrative way of calculating the ecological footprint is to convert it into global hectares, a measure that seems suitable for comparing the different regions in which humankind lives. Since 1994, this method has been used to determine biological resources, which lie primarily in renewable biological processes.[45]

Nonrenewable resources such as oil and the extraction of minerals or built-up sand are tied up in consumption and thus withdrawn from future cycles. Renewable biological resources, on the other hand, can be used productively and ensure the survival of humanity in the future. In particular, they enter the cycles again and again through continuous regrowth or biological reproduction. Scarcity of resources through extensive depletion and waste is an extensive research topic in its own right.[46]

There are calculations that describe this consumption as an ecological footprint in the Earth Overshoot Day.[47] The largest negative footprints of individual countries start as early as February. The richer the countries are, the earlier more is consumed than can be regrown. In 2019, the point from which more was consumed than could be regrown was reached after an average of seven months – the world's population lives on Earth as if it were 1.75 times present. Rich countries consume three to four times the earth in a single year. Since this development is growing, the point of overuse is being pushed forward faster and faster, so it is being reached earlier and earlier. Or, to put it another way, people have less and less time to reverse this development at all without turning the existing economic and lifestyle system completely upside down.

The calculations show that humanity has been overusing the planet's biocapacity for several decades, the richer more than the poorer. The planetary boundaries have already been exceeded, especially in terms of biodiversity loss (species extinction), nitrogen and phosphorus cycles, and climate change.[48]

One weakness of the footprint approach is that it does not fit all biological factors, such as water use and biodiversity, because it takes an area-based approach. Likewise, it is very problematic that a quantitative calculation often comes before a qualitative one. Thus, monocultural agriculture, which intensively cultivates land, is weighted better in terms of area than organic agriculture, which has a higher land consumption due to its quality. Above all, the nonbiological factors such as increasing waste, the disappearance of nonrenewable resources, the increase of toxic and long-term destructive substances in air, soil, and water are also not sufficiently included in the ecological footprint. However, they are part of a negative footprint, which we always should use as an all-encompassing term to refer to all these effects for the sake of simplicity. But it should not be omitted that there is yet no sufficient scientific methodology to comprehensively calculate it. This alone shows how, on the one hand, the representation of this phenomenon reaches the limits of complexity, but that, on the other hand, this has not yet led to a sufficiently comprehensive promotion of worldwide research efforts and to a unification of measurement standards. Basically, science would have to be developed comprehensively in such a way that realistic models of the survey of the actual state and the prognosis of further change are worked out independent of the economic and political wishful thinking in comprehensive freedom of research, publishing, and teaching. At present, freedom is granted only to a limited extent because research funds are almost always linked to economic desires.

The constructors of the ecological footprint unapologetically admit such weaknesses in their studies, but even the simplistic model already sufficiently shows that humanity is irreversibly limiting life in the future for subsequent generations far beyond the available biocapacity.

The Anthropocene is the epoch in which humankind became the most important factor influencing geological, biological, and atmospheric processes on the earth. Climate change shows that the regulating and regenerating forces of nature are becoming unbalanced, forests are dying or being cut down, although it is very clear that they could mitigate the greenhouse effect. Today, it would still be possible to reverse this destructive trend, especially through a massive reforestation program. The biggest obstacle, however, is that the world's general ownership of forests has long since been converted into private property, whose owners find it difficult to commit themselves to sustainability because the main aim is to make a profit. Biomass can renew itself, as it does in nature, but profit motives are directed at quick profits through high exploitation. Thus, the purity of water and soil fertility are diminishing due to overfertilization. In addition, factory farming, deforestation, land and soil compaction, and other factors are adding up and having an increasingly negative impact on development. In contrast, technologies of regeneration and environmentally friendly production can only mitigate the negative trend but so far have not been able to reverse it. The climate targets we miss today will be with us for centuries.

What is required of humanity in sustainability is more than defeating climate change. The depletion of nonrenewable resources, the poisoning and littering of the world, the extinction of species, the densification and sealing of the earth, as well as a massive armament with destructive weapons, are factors of the sustainability crisis, each of which in itself poses an immense threat to survival. Against this background, sustainability is by no means just a question of moving away from fossil fuels, as important as the CO_2 issue is for limiting climate change in the present.[49] Today, we are dealing with a great many areas and fields of sustainability, as shown earlier, all of which are developing their own dynamics. The idea of sustainability is a construct that focuses on a concern for nature, ecology, the environment, and human behavior. At the same time, it is also a concern for the future of humanity.

If humanity commits itself to work for sustainability – there are UN recommendations for its implementation[50] – then a normative imperative is generated to which all would have to commit: "Always act in such a way that the consequences of your actions are not to the detriment of humanity and the environment in the future." However, such a general recommendation, even if it would be approved by global governments, must always be translated into local law and concrete applications to achieve verifiable effects. Here it is necessary to understand the distinction between the terms "sustainability" and "sustainable development." Many people want to combine the two so that they don't have to completely question their previous ways of life.[51]

On the one hand, sustainability can only be achieved through radical changes in behavior. The environment would have to be protected independently of human needs and expectations of prosperity in such a way that the described challenges could be overcome.

On the other hand, there is the desire for sustainable development: Thus, national and international bodies as representatives of humanity assume that a majority wants the achieved prosperity and the previous life in abundance to be continued and perpetuated by scientific-technological progress. Many people hope that the contradiction between the necessary limitation of the harmful effects and increasing prosperity can be solved. The expectation that this can and must be achieved is overly high, the doubt about this claim is relatively low.[52] Politicians, especially in rich countries, shy away from any doubt here because it could weaken the economy and directly cost votes for all parties.[53]

The idea of development is guided by the central assumption that either a scientific and technological solution to environmental issues can be found through economic interests or a balance can be achieved in a "green economy" in social and ecological terms.[54] From the social side, which is also a part of sustainability, it is clear that in addition to the increasing ecological problems, there is a growing poverty gap between individuals in all nations and between nations, especially north and south, showing the human future as a social way of life in high inconsistency. But this interpretation of development is reconstructed quite differently in the dominant economy. The economy with its pursuit of profit, with simultaneous unjust distribution, has so far always taken precedence in capitalist strategies because – regarding the threat that is proclaimed – without it, everything would collapse anyway. Prosperity and abundance are the way to gain the favor of the masses and to save established structures, gains, and political elites.

In contrast, the worldwide poverty and wealth reports show how unequally and unfairly the world's wealth is distributed.[55] Moreover, environmental research has demonstrated that the world's rich contribute significantly more to the damage than the poor[56]: From 1990 to 2015, the richest 10 percent of the world's population blew more than twice as much climate-damaging carbon dioxide emissions into the air as the poorer half of humanity combined. One percent of the rich accounts for 15 percent of greenhouse gases, while the poorer half of humanity accounts for just 7 percent. What's more, the rich, with their SUVs and air travel, have increasingly become role models for the classes below them.

Notes

1 Cf. Caradonna, J. L. (2014): *Sustainability. A History*. Oxford/New York: Oxford University Press. A problem-based introduction can be found here: Thomas, S. A. (2016): *The Nature of Sustainability*. Grand Rapids, Michigan: Chapbook Press. In view of the social sciences: Redclift, M. (Hg.) (2005): *Sustainability. Critical Concepts in the Social Sciences*. 4 Vol. London: Routledge.
2 Carson, R. (1962): *Silent Spring*. Boston: Houghton Mifflin.
3 Cf. Crutzen, P. (2002): Geology of Mankind. In: *Nature* 415, 23. Further insightful introductions can be found, e.g., in: Davies, J. (2016): *The Birth of the Anthropocene*. Oakland: University of California Press; Hornborg, A. (2019): *Nature, Society, and Justice in the Anthropocene*. Cambridge and New York: Cambridge University Press; Scranton, R. (2015): *Learning to Die in the Anthropocene*. San Francisco: City Lights Books; Bonneuil, C. & Fressoz, J.-B. (2015): *The Shock of the Anthropocene*. The Earth, History and us. London: Verso; Lever-Tracy, C. (Ed.). (2010): *Routledge Handbook on Climate Change and Society*. London: Routledge.
4 Meadows, D. H., et al. (1972): *The Limits to Growth*. New York: Universe Books.

5 Particularly clearly and sharply analyzed in two books: Hamilton, C. (2010): *Requiem for a Species. Why We Resist the Truth About Climate Change*. Crows Nest, NSW: Allen & Unwin. And Hamilton, C. (2017): *Defiant Earth. The Fate of Humans in the Anthropocene*. Cambridge: Polity.

6 Worster, D. (2016): *Shrinking the Earth. The Rise and Decline of American Abundance*. New York: Oxford University Press.

7 Since the 1960s, the term "environment" in its various meanings has been associated with ecology movements. Nature is also often spoken of synonymously. The many possible uses of these terms gain a clear focus in sustainability when looking at the limits of nonsustainable development in very concrete terms.

8 See Jucker, R. (2014): *Do We Know What We Are Doing? Reflections on Learning, Knowledge, Economics, Community and Sustainability*. Newcastle: Cambridge Scholars Publishing, p. 49.

9 In 2021, there was more CO_2 than ever before despite the corona crisis production constraints, with particularly large increases, cf. https://www.co2.earth/

10 On the great acceleration, see footnote 14; also Davies (2016) in footnote 3 and Hamilton (2017) in footnote 4.

11 Meadows et al. footnote 4. See also Strauss, M. (2012): Looking Back on the Limits of Growth. Forty years after the release of the groundbreaking study, were the concerns about overpopulation and the environment correct? *Smithsonian Magazine*, April 2021. https://www.smithsonianmag.com/science-nature/looking-back-on-the-limits-of-growth-125269840/ and data from Stockholm Resilience Centre (2009): Planetary Boundaries Research. https://www.stockholmresilience.org/research/planetary-boundaries.html; IPBES (2019): Global Assessment Report on Biodiversity and Ecosystem Services. https://www.ipbes.net/global-assessment. See also https://www.ipcc.ch/

12 Meadows et al. footnote 4, p. 23.

13 See Stockholm Resilience Centre (2009): Planetary Boundaries Research. https://www.stockholmresilience.org/research/planetary-boundaries.html; Rockström, J., Steffen, W., Noone, K., Persson, Å., et.al. (2009): A Safe Operating Space for Humanity. *Nature*, 461, 472–475; IPBES (2019): Global Assessment Report on Biodiversity and Ecosystem Services. https://www.ipbes.net/global-assessment

14 Steffen, W., Broadgate, W., Deutsch, L., Gaffney, O., & Ludwig, C. (2015): The Trajectory of the Anthropocene: The Great Acceleration. *The Anthropocene Review* 2(1), 81–98.

15 Bello, W. (2013): *Capitalism's Last Stand? Deglobilalization in the Age of Austerity*. London, New York: Zed Books, p. 179 ff.

16 http://www.fao.org/publications/sofa/2019/en/

17 Footnote 4, p. 29.

18 Neukom, R., Barboza, L. A., Erb, M. P., et al. (2019): Consistent Multidecadal Variability in Global Temperature Reconstructions and Simulations Over the Common Era. *Nature Geoscience*, 12, 643–649.

19 A profound analysis is given by Incropera, F. P. (2016): *Climate Change: A Wicked Problem: Complexity and Uncertainty at the Intersection of Science, Economics, Politics, and Human Behavior*. New York: Cambridge University Press.

20 Cf. Dhiman, S. (2018): To Eat or Not to Eat Meat. In: Dhiman, S. & Marques, J. (Hg.): *Handbook of Engaged Sustainability*. Springer International Publishing.

21 Reasons against fish industry are summarized here. https://animalequality. org/blog/2019/09/30/fishing-industry-destroying-environment/

22 Cf. https://weltrisikobericht.de/english/

23 Incropera footnote 19, p. 89 f.

24 Incropera ibid, p. 94 ff.

25 Cf., e.g., Robock, A. (2008): 20 Reasons Why Geoengineering May Be a Bad Idea. *Bulletin of the Atomic Scientists*, Bd. 64, Nr. 2, Mai/Juni, 14–18; Schneider, S. H. (2010): Geoengineering: Could We or Should We Make It Work? In: Launder, B. E./Thompson, J. M. T. *(Hg.): Geo-Engineering Climate Change. Environmental Necessity or Pandora's Box?* Cambridge: Cambridge University Press, 3–26.

26 Incropera in footnote 19, p. 134.

27 See   https://www.climate-transparency.org/wp-content/uploads/2020/11/ Climate-Transparency-Report-2020.pdf

28 Footnote 19, p. 25 and 29. See also https://cds.climate.copernicus.eu/#!/home

29 Mauch, C. (2019): Slow Hope. Rethinking Ecologies of Crisis and Fear. *RCC Perspectives*, (1), 1–43, published by Rachel Carson Center, p. 8 f.

30 Cf., e.g., Foer, J. S. (2009): *Eating Animals*. New York: Little Brown and Company.

31 The following analyses are helpful as examples: Sassen, S. (2001): *The Global City*. New York, London, Tokyo: Princeton University Press. Megacities have to be analyzed in context of the global development: Sassen, S. (1998): *Globalization and Its Discontents*. New York: New Press; Sassen, S. (2007): *A Sociology of Globalization*. New York: W.W. Norton; Sassen, S. (2008): *Territory, Authority, Rights. From Medieval to Global Assemblages*. New York, London, Tokyo: Princeton University Press; Sassen, S. (2014): *Expulsions. Brutality and Complexity in the Global Economy*. Cambridge, MA: Harvard University Press/Belknap Book.

32 Levermann, A., et al. (2020): Projecting Antarctica's Contribution to Future Sea Level Rise from Basal Ice Shelf Melt Using Linear Response Functions of 16 Ice Sheet Models (LARMIP-2). *Earth System Dynamics*, 2020(11), 35–76.

33 The following statements are taken from the institute's website. https:// www.pik-potsdam.de/en

34 See OA–ICC – Ocean Acidification International Coordination Center (2020): Ocean Acidification. http://ocean-acidification.net/

35 See Kolbert, E. (2015): *The Sixth Extinction*. New York: Picador, 114.

36 Netflix has attempted to document the dramatic consequences of fishing in the video *Seaspiracy*. Even if some aspects are presented in a dramatized way, one truth remains at the core: The commercial interests of fishing accelerate the decline of the oceans. The world community has so far been standing idly by.

37 See Ellen Macarthus Foundation (2016): The New Plastics Economy. https://www.ellenmacarthurfoundation.org/assets/downloads/publications/NPEC-Hybrid_English_22-11-17_Digital.pdf

38 What will happen as a consequence of all these developments is being discussed, for example, by Wallace-Wells, D. (2019): *The Uninhabitable Earth. Life After Warming*. New York: Tim Duggan Books.

39 See footnote 34.

40 https://ipbes.net/global-assessment

41 Various expert panels believe that the sixth mass extinction in the history of life has already begun. According to Paul Crutzen, the Anthropocene is characterized by the following features (Crutzen footnote 3, Kolbert footnote 35, p. 108): More than anything else, humans have triggered a greenhouse effect through the use of fossil fuels that is causing open-ended climate change; between one-third and one-half of the Earth's surface has been transformed and used by humans; many nonrenewable resources are being exploited and will no longer be available in the future; most of the earth's rivers have been dammed or diverted; fertilizer crops produce more nitrogen than can be naturally absorbed by the earth's ecosystem; fisheries take more than one-third of the primary production in coastal waters; humans use more than half of the fresh water for their needs and withdraw it from ecological cycles.

42 Lovejoy, T. E. & Hannah, L. (Eds.): *Biodiversity and Climate Change. Transforming the Biosphere*. New Haven and London: Yale University Press.

43 Chivian, E. & Bernstein, A. (Eds.) (2008): *Sustaining Life. How Human Health Depends on Biodiversity*. New York: Oxford University Press.

44 All data from Sipri Yearbook (2019): *Armaments, Disarmament and International Security*. https://www.sipriyearbook.org

45 For methodology, see, e.g., Borucke, M. et al. (2013): Accounting for Demand and Supply of the Biosphere's Regenerative Capacity. The National Footprint Accounts Underlying Methodology and Framework. *Ecological Indicators*, 24(2013), 518–533; Global Footprint Network (2013): Methodology for Calculating the Ecological Footprint of California. https://www.footprintnetwork.org/content/images/article_uploads/EcologicalFootprintCalifornia_Method_2013. pdf?_ga=2.88224092.695390651.1627914510-621845368.1627914510

46 Cf. Jonsson, F. A., Brewer, J., Fromer, N., & Trentmann, F. (2019): *Scarcity in the Modern World. History, Politics, Society and Sustainability 1800–2075*. London: Bloomsbury.

47 Earth Overshoot Days Org (2019): Earth Overshoot Days 2019. https://www.overshootday.org/newsroom/country-overshoot-days/2019_country_overshoot_days-1000/

48 For the latest data, see also Stockholm Resilience Centre in footnote 13, a page that is constantly updated.

49 Cf. Malm, A. (2016): *Fossil Capital. The Rise of Steam Power and the Roots of Global Warming*. London: Verso; Mitchell, T. (2013): *Carbon Democracy. Political Power in the Age of Oil*. Second Edition. London: Verso.

50 United Nations (2016): Transforming Our World: The 2030 Agenda for Sustainable Development.

51 Allevato, E. (2018): The Spirit of Sustainability. The Fourth Dimension of the Bottom Line. In: Dhiman, S. & Marques, J. (Eds.): *Handbook of Engaged Sustainability*. Springer International Publishing, 12, suggests that in such a notion, there is always already an anthropocentric, a human prejudice, because it grasps nature only from the perspective of human actions and desires for feasibility. Dhiman, S. (2018): Selfishness, Greed, and Apathy. In: Dhiman, S. & Marques, J. (ibid.), also emphasizes that we must first understand the negative footprint we leave in the world, which

for him means above all taking a holistic view of the world and not always wanting to immediately humanize everything and turn it into business. Even if quite a few authors, such as Griggs, D., et al. (2013): Sustainable Development Goals for People and Planet. *Nature*, 495, 305–307, have the protection of the earth's conservation systems in mind, most of them still assume economic feasibility in their solutions at the same time. If this is endangered, all strategies seem to be pointless.

52 See, e.g., Frey, R. S., Gellert, P. K., & Dahms, H. F. (Eds.) (2019): *Ecologically Unequal Exchange: Environmental Injustice in Comparative and Historical Perspective.* Houndmills, UK: Palgrave Macmillan.

53 In 1987, the guiding goal of sustainable development was established at the UN level by a panel of experts as essential for world politics. The Brundtland-Report (1987): Development and International Economic Co-Operation. https://en.wikisource.org/wiki/Brundtland_Report has since expressed in particular the economic desire to be able to generate further prosperity from the sustainability agenda. In 1992, the Rio Conference of the Parties on Environment and Development took place, and Agenda 21 was developed. The follow-up conferences in Johannesburg in 2002 and Rio +20 in 2012 further developed the sustainability agenda, with the idea of global goals, the sustainable development goals, defining the 2030 Agenda. In all of these proposals, there is a prevailing optimism about being able to pursue human progress. Less close attention is paid to the obstacles.

54 UNEP (2011): *Towards Green Economy. Pathways to Sustainable Development and Poverty Eradication.* United Nations Environmental Programme. https://sustainabledevelopment.un.org/content/documents/126GER_synthesis_en.pdf

55 It has even become more and more significant over the years: Freeland, C. (2012): *Plutocrats. The Rise of the New Global Super-Rich.* London: Penguin; to understand the background: Stiglitz, J. (2012): *The Price of Inequality. How Today's Divided Society Endangers Our Future.* London: W.W. Norton & Company; Stiglitz, J. (2015): *The Great Divide.* New York: Norton; Ferguson, N. (2008): *The Ascent of Money. A financial History of the World.* New York: Penguin; Higgens, K. L. (2015): *Economic Growth and Sustainability. Systems Thinking for a Complex World.* San Diego, US: Elsevier Academic Press.

56 Oxfam (2020): Confronting Carbon Inequality. Putting Climate Justice at the Heart of the COVID-19 Recovery. https://www.oxfam.de/system/files/documents/20200921–confronting–carbon–inequality.pdf

2 Causes

How Did We Get into the Crisis?

Why Is a Lack of Sustainability So Deeply Rooted in Human Behavior?

Already in the early advanced civilizations, an individualization of human activities has taken place that has started with an abundance of products for living. As soon as people differed in their prosperity, the ego began to seek its advantages, to assert its possessions, its security, its privileged sexuality and offspring, its status against others. All means are right for her or him to get what is necessary for this.[1] In the struggle for survival, patterns of competition have developed. They continue to have an effect on civilization. The more prosperity grows, the fewer moral models restrict the delimited human being in his or her boundless desires. What is missing, in particular, is a general successful education for a sustainable common good. But recently, the sustainability crisis has become unmistakably visible; the conditions that created it have been in place for a long time. The boundless, immoderate, and ruthless lifestyle against other people and nature is the result of the success story of modern society, which has intensified since the middle of the 20th century.[2]

But there is also a countermovement against human shortsightedness and ruthlessness. Exuberant desires are at least in part restrained by social coexistence, shaped by cooperation and communication so that pure chaos, arbitrariness, and encroachment do not dominate unchallenged. A moderation of lusts, a prudence brought about by educational and governmental measures, and, in more recent times, a policy of social compensation are regarded as prerequisites for human coexistence, for respecting the diverse community and others, for not doing to anyone what one does not want to experience oneself.

In this social situation, an age of individualization has been driven by capitalism, which strongly emphasizes personal advantages. The

DOI: 10.4324/9781003276449-2

repeatedly invoked achievements of successful people and nations are often mentioned in key words: Self-initiative; daring; perseverance; strength; striving for power and expansion in order to increase; pride in achievements, in accomplishments – local and national – prosperity; and abundance, which can also drive arts and aesthetics, architecture, sciences, and academies. But above all, and again and again, the courage to act and to do.[3] A nation's achieved prosperity is also associated with the power of its assertiveness against other countries, people, and the planet. This forms social and national affiliations that can be enforced by celebrating one's own greatness in order to overlook one's own weaknesses in belittling others. Today, these mostly unquestioned advantages have turned into risks for the planet.[4]

The disadvantages for the less successful people are also recurring: Few benefit, others are left behind, exploited, have to go to wars, are the first to be sacrificed, and are always discriminated against as lazy, comfortable, unworthy, cowardly, poor, or otherwise. They belong, but they are insignificant.[5] They participate less directly in progress but are still part of the progress story propagated on all sides.

Today, as the earth's resources have been dynamically exploited, as the climate becomes hotter and the water more polluted, as land becomes scarcer and housing more expensive, as work and prosperity become more uncertain in the face of a variety of environmental problems and social contradictions, we must make new calculations.[6]

Societies, it has become very clear in the course of human history, must always adapt their success to changing conditions, either from outside or from their internal development. They must be able to address their own sustainability. If they fail to do so, they are doomed sooner or later[7] because they may discuss contradictions from outside or from within, but they can only resolve them if they consistently change and adapt their behavior to the challenges of their environment.

The Unsustainable Agenda of the Occident

Europe, as the cradle of capitalism, has carried it out into the world. In the process, a worldview emerged that many people today have adopted. The attitude behind it was formulated very clearly by Niccolò Machiavelli, and it is quite simple:[8] There are no eternal states, no eternal walls or durable borders, everything is determined by the struggle of all against all. Any ideology that wants to explain the world to us is merely an instrument of this struggle. All actions – regardless of their justification – are always declarations of struggle: First act, then justify. Lies, crimes of all kinds, are formed according to the following patterns: Don't do it if the superiority is too great. If it is not too great, then do it and apologize. If there is no other way, do it and deny the crime. In any case, do it and do not regret it because what you do not do, someone else will.

If we look at the struggle for sustainability, then environmental sins, in particular, seem to be well explainable along the lines of Machiavelli. Let's take the exemplary example of glyphosate at Monsanto or today Bayer: Don't spray the poison if the regulations become too strong or high fines force you to do so. Justify yourself through pseudo-scientists who deny everything. Or, if that doesn't help, excuse yourself through compensation that you simultaneously declare unjustified. Deny the damage and just move on – because if you don't, someone else will.

Machiavelli may be too simple for many. But sometimes it is necessary to simplify in order to get an overview and to focus on existential questions. The state or rule in today's capitalism does not have to be just according to well-founded values, but they are measured by utility and profits. The profits are sufficient if they reach particularly influential people, who can influence opinions. Thus, there is a power of the factual: In capitalist reality, violence, or violations, are not divided according to good and evil, but primarily according to success and usefulness – measured in the amount of money owned.

The newly emerging markets of bourgeois society, which determine the value of human beings by the price they can fetch on their markets, force everyone into a tacit agreement. In a democracy, the state with its organs is accepted because it creates a framework for freedom in return: Freedom of choice, freedom of expression, freedom of self-realization, freedom of consumption. Only the flip side of this freedom is always the money that someone has to raise in order to afford his freedoms.[9] Therefore, the degree of power exercised and the chance to enjoy libertarian rights is very differently distributed by the possession of money in the world.[10] And the forgotten side is the damage that all the freedoms mean in terms of the boundaries of the earth.

Money alone does not guarantee freedom indefinitely. In dictatorships, people are deprived of freedom of expression and free elections. In despotic regimes, such as China, Russia, and Turkey at present, human rights are restricted and freedoms curtailed. And with that, also the chances to be able to work freely and unrestrictedly for sustainability.

Growth, Power, Money

As far as prosperity and growth are concerned, it is always the better-off who benefit first, but in the affluent countries, more and more people are able to participate. Prosperity and growth have increased steadily in recent decades, and the effects of these developments are expressed in the growing negative footprint of rich countries in particular. Countries interested in national economic growth tend to overlook the consequences of the lack of sustainability because growth is seen as the ever-functioning currency of progress and any abandonment threatens it. Growth accelerates all production and life processes, leaving ecosystems unprotected because they incur costs, reduce profits, and do not themselves contribute to growth in easy ways.

The thinking and imagination trap we are in with regard to sustainability consists – in a world determined by money – above all in our desire for prosperity and individual security, and the idea of an economy that allows infinite consumption. It is accompanied by a state that drives this while protecting it nationally. Many people believe that within an anarchy of markets it is right to act selfishly, while at the same time hoping that the economy and the state will protect them from all risks when in doubt.

To strengthen these supposedly protective systems, priority is then usually given to economic growth over the social question, which today, full of conflict, still affects even the rich countries. In addition, as a legacy of civil societies, nature and the environment appear to them to be infinitely large and therefore endlessly usable – capable of coping with all human demands.

Liberalism as a Delimited Way of Life

Science, technology, and, above all, the economy still follow a liberal conception. The state appears as the administrator of a common interest, as the administrator of infrastructures that are supposed to keep everything going. Scientific-technological progress in capitalist production requires enormous resources, consumes energies, and produces waste in inconceivable quantities. The breadth and consequences of such actions are accepted because progress seems to be necessary and, moreover, to serve everyone. The economy pushes for everything from which profits can be made. This approach is never designed for the long term; it is always measured in terms of short-term success – i.e., profits. Most of the time, there is no sense of the consequences that affect health in the long run, for example, or that only later generations will have to bear as environmental consequences. If raw materials are lacking later, then this is not our problem. The state should first and foremost organize prosperity for as many as possible in the here and now.

Historically, it first secures the prerogatives of successful nations as a nation-state through conflicts and wars; later, it acts through its economic power and its political and military influence. The abundance produced and sold in the markets is considered the hallmark of a successful state.

Through this incessant striving, people increasingly lose the idea of a greater meaning of life that could be thought beyond the increase of material wealth and consumer goods. They focus primarily on what is feasible: The conquest of those resources that can satisfy the ever-increasing needs and generate ever-new ones, triggering an insatiable hunger for power over anything that promises a high yield for selfish motives. This happens for the individual life, as well as for the national aspiration. The liberal state is left only with the task of preventing excessive greed, unrestricted criminality, the non-observance of contracts, the violation of legal and contractual relationships, and the endangering of private property. Actually, sustainability should also be part of this program today, but it has not yet arrived in the consciousness of the majority as a general endangerment of humanity and its possessions.

The Inequality of People Is Growing

The poor and the rich are divided everywhere, and this division is constantly increasing.[11] The level of wealth in rich countries and the resulting environmental burdens are steadily rising, while most of humanity struggles to survive in poverty.

People's perceptions are always influenced by the system in which they live: Capitalism has prevailed worldwide; alternatives are hardly imaginable. Everywhere there is a liberal view of economics and property, which has driven people into unimaginable and growing inequality. Today, even democratic and despotic countries work together, whereby the democracies, through the markets, strengthen the very despots they should basically despise. And a second contradiction appears: The gap between rich and poor is growing in all countries, as are the differences between rich and poor countries.[12]

The respective wealth gap and the different standards of living are considered natural, especially for the better-off. Why should those who have more than others want to doubt the correctness of inequality? This phenomenon is often glossed over: It is claimed that self-interest drives people to contribute to general prosperity. Liberalism, an older ideology of economic action, and neoliberalism, a newer one, are particularly reliant on this assumption and are based on a distrust of government intervention of regulation for the common good. Every time when greater taxation, limits on profiteering, environmental damage, or other social or sustainable demands are proposed, liberal voices resound, recalling capitalist principles and presenting them as the only solution. The basic idea is simple and easy to recognize: Property, which is constantly multiplied, is the sun that forms the core of all selective interests, around which all planets of human desires are supposed to revolve in an order of constant growth that seems to be governed by natural law.

The Decline of the Common Good

The social contract, whether we are conscious of it or simply live it, says that to secure and increase their property, people should do whatever increases their wealth, whatever is achievable through struggles of conquest and distribution, no matter what it costs others or how it harms the planet.[13] Property establishes inequality. It also always goes hand in hand with lack of freedom, because as soon as I own something, it belongs to me and therefore no longer to the others. I then say in this sense, "Here, at this fence, your freedom ends! No trespassing!" From the point of view of ownership, the perspective narrows more and more because from now on costs and damages to one's own property are to be avoided. As long as immediate catastrophes do not endanger one's property, dangers to the common good are readily forgotten. The liberal way of thinking and the thought patterns programmed for growth are drives that want to shape the world only for their own benefit. Constant growth is equated with human self-preservation. Economics and politics are particularly well suited to spreading narratives about this, and it seems they have no alternative. If democracy, which is based on the separation of powers, is emphasized by many today as the best constitution of humanity, it must always be remembered that private property has been unequally distributed from the beginning. The inequality inherent in it has been compensated for with the affluent society since the middle of the 20th century in the rich industrialized countries by an increase in the relative wealth of many people, which means that while some own more and more, the masses are at least enabled to have a certain standard of living. However, the costs of sustainability must be borne by all people. In light of the liberal economic view, the damage caused today by cost avoidance in all areas to the environment and nature, to the health and burden of the population, is not paid in the first place by the polluters and perpetrators, the winners and profiteers, but is charged to humanity as a whole. People are comforted with the eternal mantra of capitalism that the surplus values from profit maximization also bring more prosperity for the general public. Either they are not educated enough to see behind the obscure figures of the rich who make everything look good or they are not determined enough to do something about it as long as they are relatively well-off.

Today, rights are distributed and laid down in comprehensive laws; ownership is regulated; a society of continuous profit maximization is constructed. It is a world of imagination with a broad consensus to live in the best of all worlds and not have to change anything. This world includes the bargain hunter up to the manager in the corporation with shareholder value, whereby everyone always has only his own profit in mind. Within this liberal market logic, three demands are almost always solved in the following patterns that favor the benefits for the haves:

First, in liberalism, the lower classes are to be protected by a pronounced social security system only to the extent that is absolutely necessary. Thus, demands for more social justice or unrest are to be avoided since the costs of such protection would come out of one's own profits – for example, through higher wages, company shareholdings, health care.

Second, the protection of nature or the environment should also be avoided because here, too, costs have to be raised, which reduces one's own profits. If not preventable, all people should bear these burdens equally so that the profits are preserved; in the principle of equality, politics willingly follows this claim.

Third, the idea of common property, a commons, or land owned in common by all has to be abandoned. Therefore, rarely is the rich factory owner's park made available to the public; usually, people lack freely accessible space in their neighborhoods, exacerbating social inequalities. If you want a beautiful and natural world, you have to be able to afford green space and living.

Why Is a Lack of Sustainability Preferred?

Against the backdrop of the initial situation just described in simplified terms, there are a number of factors that promote a lack of sustainability. The following aspects are dynamically intertwined:

The Power of Selfishness

The human capacity to achieve material prosperity has steadily increased throughout history. Those in possession want to retain, increase, and defend this prosperity and the security that goes with it. Against demands for moderation or renunciation, they therefore quickly develop defensive reactions to protect their own views: If I'm doing well, if I own property, an apartment or a house, maybe even a nice garden that I water regularly, if business is good, in other words, if I'm completely satisfied, why should I change anything in my life? My resistance grows immediately if something is to be taken away from me. I revolt if I no longer get the water for my garden consistently – I pay for it — I do not see at all that my car, my boat, my travels, my meat, and all that I value in life in abundance should now all at once be regulated, limited, priced. Didn't people fight for centuries for this freedom of theirs, and now I'm just supposed to give it away without defense?[14]

The Ecological Burdens of Wealth

As has already been pointed out, rich people cause much more green-house gases and damage to the earth's borders than poorer people. "The richest one percent of the world's population are responsible for more than twice as much carbon pollution as the 3.1 billion people who made up the poorest half of humanity during a critical 25-year period of unprecedented emissions growth… Annual emissions grew by 60 percent between 1990 and 2015. The richest 5 percent were responsible for over a third (37 percent) of this growth. The total increase in emissions of the richest one percent was three times more than that of the poorest 50 percent."[15]

Compared to poor countries, rich countries generate higher eco-burdens. Poor countries are always doubly affected: First, their raw materials and labor are exploited, and then they are expected to bear the consequences of climate change and all the global damage. The humanity of the rich countries is proclaimed again and again, but little of the human promise for an equal life is actually realized for all.

Clearly, the rich would have to shoulder significantly more burdens. Why doesn't the state of rich countries regulate in this sense? Why is there no sufficient pricing and taxation here? Because there are too many nonsustainable people in politics? Because there are too many nonsustainable people at the election who would punish such decisions?

Unjustly, however, even when it comes to paying in rich countries, everyone is to be charged equally. The principle of equality is often invoked in democracy when it comes to the distribution of costs so as not to diminish unequal profits. Then what happens is what has been shown with the energy levy, that consumers have to help pay for the discount for industry via the electricity price. This is an economic policy that deprives polluters and burdens the general public. This is a policy of the nonsustainable for the gains of polluters and a lack of sustainability for the public.[16]

Sustainability Is Not Enforceable

Although some responsible parties can be clearly identified, the question of who is responsible for the lack of sustainability is often difficult to clarify precisely: In an age of individualization, everyone leaves a footprint in this world that is more or less harmful. But individuals are always part of a social group, a community at the local level, a municipality that is more or less committed to sustainability. They are part of a country, a nation, which has enacted laws for or against the environment and nature but most of the time does not even provide for a basic right to an intact and protected environment, a healthy environment that sustains life. Sustainability has so far been so decisively excluded worldwide that it is not legally enforceable! Thus, even if individuals support sustainability and want to advocate for it, they are limited in their options. This is reflected in many concrete questions: How do I get to work, if not by car? How sustainable can I make my living space? How can I feed myself in sustainable ways? And what about the waste, the pollutants, the burdens on the environment? What can I control and improve, and who will help me?[17]

If you take a closer look at such questions, it quickly becomes clear: The lack of sustainability is driven by an economy that wants to sell because it can earn money on climate-damaging goods by glossing over emissions standards and directly cheating.[18] An economy that incentivizes consumption, fixated on the good and the sale, but not on what the consequences are. That does not penalize when waste is produced and numerous pollutants are rising in consumption. The merely profit-oriented economy is not a driver of a sustainable world. Moreover, it is supported by a neoliberal policy that lets the markets get away with almost everything so that it looks good nationally. In such kind of wishful thinking, this process is enforced day by day; humanity thinks and acts shortsightedly again and again. A policy that does not want to look at the world scientifically and soberly but is only oriented toward its own wishes and next election results, will not be able to point the way to a healthy future. And consumers who trust that they will always receive something good, high quality because they are paying, remain naïve in the face of a reality whose dangers they do not foresee because they put their egoistic satisfaction above all other questions.

Sustainability Denial

As a result of climate change, the major fires in the last years reveal that the sustainability crisis has long since arrived in rich countries as well. The fires in the USA and Australia were the start of what is to come. And in the Amazon, fires are being deliberately caused to open up land for agriculture for the benefit of rich countries in particular. The increase in greenhouse gases from these fires is enormous. The economic consequences can still be assessed regionally here, but all ecological impacts are global.[19] Who pays for the damages? Who punishes the polluters? The nonsustainable government – e.g., in Australia, a country still politically committed to fossil fuels – does not identify causes, but claims that the bushfires are mere coincidence: Aren't bushfires part of the natural course of events? At what point is it appropriate to speak of an impact of the climate crisis? At what point is it time for majorities and nations to turn to scientific insights? At what point does the world intervene when the Amazon, the lungs of the world, are being destroyed?[20]

The Contradiction between Knowledge and Behavior

The example of reducing one's own negative footprint is a good illustration of another problem: There is a clear gap between knowledge and behavior; ecological attitudes rarely lead to actual sustainable behavior.[21] To change one's own footprint, the gap between intention and actual action must always be overcome. This gap is maintained especially when social pressure from like-minded people is not strong enough for more sustainability. For example, when Donald Trump denied climate change as president of the United States, it had an impact on those who actually acknowledge climate change but traditionally vote Republican. One's own intentions are always shaped by the environment and are influenced by prevailing practices. The less the government regulation of sustainability is and when punishment through costs for harmful polluters is low, the less the necessary social pressure can form for more sustainability in the broad population. Thus, while each is responsible for its own sustainability, this cannot sufficiently work without sustainable policies and a government with sustainable agendas.[22] Human behavior in this sense is very much dependent on a positive narrative about the need for sustainable action.

The Lobby of Nonsustainable People

The power of habits, like the conservative effect of the social group, creates very high barriers to behavior change. The nonsustainable are always already protected from attacks on their behavior by their seemingly successful lifestyle.[23] Those who enjoy great freedom and are satisfied with their lives are considered successful. Prosperity and wealth, abundance and superfluity seem to be an inevitable part of it.

The model of success is proclaimed and advertised everywhere, not without the influence of economic lobbies. Examples of the present sufficiently show how a few influential people, politicians, and conservative think tanks, as well as pseudo-scientific institutes, are able to influence humanity through media and advertising and to enforce their selective interests.[24] Whether it is the downplayed dangers of smoking, the use of pesticides, acid rain, greenhouse gases, nitrogen oxides, speed limits, or other dangers, the strategy is always similar: Harm is downplayed, harmful effects for people and the environment are trivialized.[25] Scientists are even found to deceive their own values and confirm anything that increases profits in exchange for good money. So-called scientific pseudo-reports are the tip of a strategy of lies and distortions because even scientific results are ultimately open to stretching and interpretation and can be a source of one's own profits through one-sided and selective interpretations.

By quite a few nonsustainable people, climate change is gladly constructed as a big conspiracy. Even scientifically educated professionals when following a conservative party line forget the facts of the ecological crisis and engage in wishful thinking. The media, which are often influenced by rich people who profit from nonsustainable conditions, also like to take advantage of this. The actual independence of the media in a country is one of the strongest indicators of the state of its democracy. It should be of great concern to all of us that this independence is steadily decreasing.

Wishful Thinking and Excuses

In today's media world, so much information is simply juxtaposed, and the existential question of sustainability is just one topic among many. It may well already be an existential issue for quite a few people, but in the pluralism of information and opinions, it cannot simply be prioritized for everyone. Thus, the unsustainable can easily reinforce their worldview by pointing out the diversity and differences in reports. Since many people want an ideal world, they like to believe they will live in such a world by employing wishful thinking for as long as possible. Most people check, for example, threatening changes of the climate by observing the actual weather in order to judge from their own observations what is actually happening. And in doing so, it is prevalent that they judge such events strongly according to desired expectations. They avoid thinking in terms of probabilities, which seems to them to be abstract and far removed from reality. They are always more influenced by the present than by a possible future, especially if this will occur more comprehensively years later, as in the case of climate change or resource depletion. In addition, they prefer a fair assessment, which initially always means that they want to be treated fairly in terms of the wealth they have achieved, what they have worked for and acquired.[26]

The Power of Little Lies

It is striking that especially the upper middle class, which can economically and socially afford to act more sustainably than others, provides most activists for climate protection and other sustainable goals. However, when behavior is then analyzed under real conditions, it becomes obvious through participant observation, as opposed to surveys, that self-perception clearly differs from the reality of behavior.[27] Many wish to be sustainable, but then don't do it consistently.

However, sustainable people more easily do recognize what will happen if they do not live and act more sustainably; they take part more easily and are shocked more quickly. But they live in a thoroughly self-contradictory world. Their home is insulated with panels that are already hazardous waste. Their natural gas heating works with condensing boiler technology and still produces too many greenhouse gases. They ask themselves, What can we use to replace fossil fuels? They need a car to get to work because mass transit is poorly developed, but some take a low-emission model. Silently, many think that greenhouse gases are produced especially by mass use to justify their small car with lower emissions. They think sustainably; for that, they become vegetarians, but is this enough when factory farming for eggs and milk, cheese, and other products still produces among other things a lot of methane? Or are they comforted when methane is degraded after about 12 years in the atmosphere, whereas CO_2 is still preserved at 15–40 percent after 1,000 years? It worries them that soy cultivation is causing the Amazon jungle to disappear: How many of their vegetarian and vegan dishes are made with soy? Where is it grown? They can't research everything, and the state does far too little to help them get an overview through transparent rules. But many people already separate their waste. And when they want to buy something, they don't always use Amazon. Some only take the car when they need to transport heavy products. Only when they get older, they will probably use it more again. They have to admit that they still want to experience a lot: Others have already seen the world, what about their world travels? Should they deny themselves what others have been allowed to do?

Who of the sustainable ones honestly wants to claim to be completely free of these statements with contradictions? Several psychological studies, not only on sustainability, show that many people in uncertain situations, where it is not immediately clear and obvious what the consequences of their actions will be, almost always tend to interpret the situation in terms of their subjective desires, interests, and personal gain. The factors with a high impact on the environment just touch central human desires. What wouldn't we have to do? Do without children, use smaller dwellings, no cars, no flights, less meat consumption. But is that what we want? Hasn't the world of prosperity promised us the exact opposite?

Against this background, we readily form a logic in which we consistently pursue the more easily attainable sustainable goals with modest behavioral changes – such as waste separation – but then omit those lifestyle changes that promise truly high effectiveness. And the little lies that consumers in rich countries use to reassure themselves become big lies when their governments announce climate packages or negotiate targets at international conferences that are ultimately all about what they can't do: They cannot simply limit, regulate, and reduce consumption. They don't want to impose that on consumers. They claim that would be socially unjust. It would be harmful to the nation, to the business location, to jobs, to everything. Setting such goals is not possible, especially if you want to be re-elected.

The mainstream economy takes the demands of the sustainability agenda in stride as long as economic development remains at the forefront of the agenda. Against this background, they even call for some action to make the economy more ecological.[28] And what has long been true for the social issue is exacerbated for ecology, because the costs should be borne by all if possible, and the gains made by as few as ever. Against this background, development becomes a kind of myth that seems to be able to unite the opposing forces of social justice and the growing economy with profit-making. And politics? Neither descriptions with mass appeal such as Al Gore's film *An Inconvenient Truth* nor the constant status reports of the Intergovernmental Panel on Climate Change (https://www.ipcc.ch/, now in its sixth reporting phase until 2022) have led to any actual radical change of course. The Glasgow COP 26 climate conference in 2021 united a majority of countries on the importance of limiting CO_2 in particular, but the unity ended immediately when it came to committing to specific actions and limits. There is even a tendency for some countries to expect benefits from not introducing the limits as quickly as others. Such nationalism leads to disaster in global warming.

How Does the Economy Prevent Sustainability?

At first glance, the modern era is a success story up to the present day: Industrialization is being pushed forward more and more – mostly at the expense of the environment – which also improves the material prosperity of people previously struggling for survival. In addition, the codification of desired behaviors is standardized in education up to regulations and laws, the securing of property and private property is legally perfected. In equal treatment, aristocratic birth privileges are renounced, but they still operate on the basis of ownership and inheritance. In the process of democratization, secret and free elections are fought for to give all people representative opportunities for equal participation. In addition, social security can be more or less realized in rich countries. The expansion of education – with elementary education for all and continuing education for a very few at first and then for more and more since the beginning of the 21st century – is progressing. Plurality and diversity are possible, there are many freedoms in society, although all advancements are regulated by school selection and opportunities for social advancement are not equally distributed. These are all particularly important points in the self-image of today. In this development, however, social justice is being transformed into a distribution struggle, with the increasing gap between rich and poor showing the one-sided distribution of gains – even in rich countries. More and more a liquefied capitalism is emerging, which is characterized by the fact that capital always migrates to those places where profits are even easier to achieve and where sustainable constraints are lowest. Against this background, it becomes clear that there is a fundamental economic denial of social equity, as well as extensive sustainability in capitalism.

The Social as the Main Problem of Sustainability

Especially in the field of economics, here in connection with the social change toward the machine and later industrially producing societies, questions of sustainability have been addressed since the 18th century. In the political economy of Adam Smith, John Stuart Mill, David Ricardo, and Thomas Robert Malthus, the limits to economic and demographic growth were problematized in view of the initial effects of the Industrial Revolution.[29] The analyses focused on questions of the interrelationships between the development of prosperity, social justice, and the dangers of overpopulation. However, since the theses at the time about the demise of societies due to overpopulation did not prove to be true and the agricultural sector was able to produce significantly more than initially thought thanks to improved methods, a long phase of forgetting about sustainable problem situations occurred. Since then, the steadily growing spread of capitalism has been dominated by a belief in progress, which over a long period of time has proven to be true in the form of actual increases in prosperity for most people.[30] However, this prosperity is distributed differently. Inequality raises the question of social justice. This question applies not only between people but also between nations. Richer countries significantly gain more wealth through colonization and exploitation. As long as the starting positions of poor countries do not change, there will hardly be any more social justice for them. But the same question also arises in the rich countries, where there are many poor people who are also disadvantaged. The whole ideology of growth that benefits all has to be questioned in capitalism.[31] But concepts of degrowth,[32] of small is beautiful,[33] and renunciations for society as a whole have always remained contentious.[34]

The Rift between Production and Consumption

This can be shown by the relationship between production and consumption: Marx already spoke of an incurable rift caused by the fact that the natural use-values produced in agriculture are separated from the place of their consumption.[35] City and countryside face each other; today, the rift by places of production and consumption pervades all consumer goods. Marx could not yet have imagined the extent and the sharpness with which this is happening. The crack also pervades the consciousness of people who more and more lose a connection to nature and to the production of their food, thus giving up the value of nature, respect for animals and plants, closeness to and appreciation of the natural environment. The crack appears when cheap goods are produced through working conditions and child labor, which the consumer wants nothing to do with but still promotes by buying cheap goods. It is this rift that underlies many of the problems of sustainability.

An Incomprehensible Increase in Money

But not only the rift created by the separation of production and consumption and the resulting alienation from nature and manufacturing but also the rift created by the way successes and profits are achieved is crucial. Capitalism relies on capital valorization. Where there is something, there should be more. Surplus values are the constant goal, even if different economic theories fundamentally argue about how such surplus values are gained. In the end, regardless of the different approaches, there is always one result: Some people who already own something generate profits in a seemingly mysterious way, which constantly multiply. The logic of this multiplication can be explained in different ways. For Marx, surplus value arises from the relationship between wage labor and capital; today, a more diverse picture of sources of surplus value production emerges: It can be generated by supply and demand, illusion, deception and fraud, or parasitic gains – such as inheritance or advancement through marriage. Commodity production stands only for a part of the profits; today, the highest surplus values come from speculation.[36]

Money is always at the center. In the age of today's dominant stock exchanges and markets, of bubbles and speculation, money multiplies much faster than the material possessions into which it can be transformed. In the process, the neoliberal economy has maximized profits in a way that must seem incomprehensible to the layman because they are increasingly made through transactions and speculations behind which there are no longer any real values or concrete, visible forms of material production at all but rather bets, projections, and profit bubbles.[37] Majorities trust today, more or less, a system that is basically incomprehensible to them – in the famously long-lived hope that at some point something will fall off for them as well.

Wealth and Sustainability Are Opposites

The wealth that is concentrated among fewer and fewer people is a threat to humanity because it is almost never linked to a sustainable way of life. Wealth and sustainability form an irreconcilable opposition; no exemplary behavior with special efforts of renunciation or ecological prudence can be derived from wealth and the resulting opportunities. The rich elites determine economic activity; they always have new business ideas to make profits. They would turn to sustainability only if it could be linked to profits or if taxes could be saved. This is one of the main challenges of economic policy in the near future.

For the sake of profit orientation, capital is increasingly being split up into global goods production with favorable production locations and into services and speculation. Cheap almost always means that cost-intensive, sustainable action is avoided. Low wages in low-wage countries, which not only affect the workers and their exploitation but also offer few future opportunities for their children, are one strategy of profit maximization, with resource exploitation and environmental damage another. To put it bluntly, the prosperity of rich countries is cofinanced by the working conditions, environmental burdens, and resource depletion imposed on poorer countries.

The self-evident way in which people live in this system and largely consider it to be without alternative makes them constantly hope for prosperity and profits, and at the same time resign themselves to the fact that the way in which the profits come about, as well as the chance to share in them, is always unequally distributed.

Social Injustice and Sustainability

Realistically, as a critical analysis of economic data shows, the broad masses have remained poor because they have little chance of achieving prosperity through low wages, part-time, and temporary work. Higher-wage groups are in a more favorable position, but compared with the richer share of the population, they are already relatively poor again. The majority will have to bear the brunt of the costs and damages of a lack of sustainability because they are comparatively much more heavily taxed than the minority of richer people. Nevertheless, a great many people still believe in the success story of today's society, no matter how much they notice the fractures and missing links in their own lives. They hold on to this belief as long as there is still a downward gradation in their own society and in relation to other countries. The tendency to relativize everything is a core concern of today's societies anyway. In terms of questions of diversity, of possible lifestyles, this is a valuable approach, but in terms of explanations of social and sustainable conditions and actions for a better life, it is often a hindrance.

Against this background, people are very concerned with their own social security. For them, sustainability in the living of humanity and the conditions of the planet is something rather abstract. It seems secondary to many because their own social security in precarious circumstances takes precedence. The liquefaction of living conditions creates pressure for constant change and constant readjustment to changing conditions. In view of the dynamics generated by this, the longing of individuals for an overview, authorities, advisers, and examples of how to successfully cope with confusion grows alongside the freedom that is always claimed. The danger that they will be exploited, manipulated, and deceived in this process is growing at the same rate.

In light of all the answer-givers of capitalist bliss, sustainability always appears as a cost to the winners. To accumulate capitalist profits, costs of any kind are to be avoided, and so either labor wages are depressed or the costs of protecting nature, the environment, and resources are simply charged to the general public. Taxes and duties as sources of income, on the other hand, have long been lowered by the capitalist economy for the rich, because they have declared to politicians their "necessary" high profits as systemically relevant, and they rake in all the benefits that can be achieved through lobbying. Moreover, many profits are diverted into speculative bubbles in order to accelerate the multiplication of money more and more.

After all, in capitalist development, the labor movement with its trade unions and social struggles has taken care of improving the social situation of working people, at least in richer countries. The situation regarding sustainability is much worse. Nature and the environment are not "unionized," they have too little political presence, and when they do appear in party platforms, compromises are quickly made so that the business location is not endangered. And since the environment imposes costs that are also directly felt by working people, for the labor movement, or what remains of it today, sustainability is also rather a secondary and even predominantly problematic issue. Working people have also recognized that the costs imposed on them by sustainability will reduce the prosperity they have already fought for. Such cost-benefit thinking, thinking that measures success only in terms of short-term profits, makes it particularly difficult to implement sustainability in the capitalist economy. It is an expression of an attitude that has become dominant, indicating that many people have lost the sense of the essential questions of their community survival.

Sustainability and Consumption Are Contradictions

Sustainability and consumption are mutually exclusive and are also valued oppositely: While consumption is everywhere and essential for people, sustainability is still very rare and controversial. People in richer countries identify themselves through consumption. Consumption is not only the basis for their standard of living but also for freedom, mobility, advancement, and all their aspirations for the rest of their lives. Increasingly, they are beginning to think in economic and political piecemeal terms and consciously lose sight of their environment.[38] The rich countries lament the poverty of the world; they deplore the climate change, but real renunciation, which could change things, appears as politically, nevertheless, not enforceable because the material being determines the horizons of consciousness, and this, in turn, judges the situation. Limiting one's life for sustainability must seem utterly nonsensical within a system in which success is measured primarily by consuming more and more. And hopes for how consumption could become more sustainable are dampened by the fact that implementation has so far been almost impossible. The majority seems not to be interested in practicing it at a higher cost.

For sustainability, the diversity and mass of consumption are fatal because for consumption, we need more and more of everything: More and more energy must be used for production and services, more and more raw materials that do not regenerate are consumed, more and more waste is produced, more and more water is used. But since it is precisely consumption that satisfies people, motivates them to work and earn money, and thus keeps economic cycles alive, a call to do without will hardly get them to vote for a party. However, this is precisely where politics should intervene boldly, but so far it does the opposite: It does not label consumer goods with regard to their sustainability, and it does not price them sufficiently. Even a warning system against unhealthy food is not in place everywhere. Too many people are too often willing to risk their health and forget about the environment. Whether vacations and travel to the places of desire are sustainable, there is no calculation method for that either. When it comes to food and leisure, the external instances of regulation of sustainability have so far been politically dismissed as particularly unreasonable, because this could upset the economy and hinder one's freedom.

Consumption differentiates individuals; it creates status, prestige, attractiveness, differences that affect both subjective feeling and social standing. Consumption is an economic machine designed so that people do not question it: It would be best for capitalism, which focuses on profit maximization, if people thought that consumption and sustainability were two completely separate matters.

To put it in a nutshell: Consumption and sustainability are fundamentally opposed when resources are consumed and not renewed, when pollutants are emitted and not compensated for, when needs are satisfied and their long-term consequences for nature, the environment, and one's own health are not considered.

Sustainability Is Secondary for the Economy

In addition, the rich have another crisis constantly in mind. They fear that the speculative real estate and financial system could collapse even sooner, before the consequences of a lack of sustainability set in.

There is little dispute among economic experts that this will happen, given the figures at hand; what is debatable is when and how it will happen and what will grow out of it as a consequence. The behavior of people shows that the short-term nature of action successes weighs much more than long-term precautions. The strategies focus mainly on high profits and quick success; they create ways of thinking and behaving that are becoming more and more dominant in our culture. If people are constantly concerned about their money and its rapid increase, there is little room for sustainable considerations. Within such a societal prioritization on money concerns, it is not surprising if there is a lack of imaginations that are future oriented and careful with resources.

Public debt is an important indicator of the dreaded crisis.[39] In just a few decades, these debts have grown exponentially in rich countries and have increased substantially again as a result of the coronavirus crisis. All citizens in rich countries are now so indebted that it is illusory to believe these debts could ever be liquidated. It even appears to many economists that it makes sense to incur as much debt as possible in order to maintain or even expand – in the short term – the prosperity of the broad masses. Here it must be considered that all debts are taken up on the financial markets; there, the money of the rich and super-rich is available in abundance, their utilization virtually calls for debts. These funds have increased because they have not been adequately siphoned off through fairer taxes. And the increasing wealth shows that the debt could be reduced in the first place if the states would change their tax models in coordination with each other. What can the state do? Reduce debt through fairer taxation. And spend the new debt on sustainability in particular. And since the majority won't be able to pay the debts that have already been created, at some point a balance will be established that will shake the existing economic and political system. Here, the rich have more to fear than the poor.

Neoliberal economists are always fighting to keep profits flowing in the here and now. Such thinking determines the politics of the present. And the political economy that emerges from it decisively defines the opportunities and limits of current sustainability. Debt in particular is readily used as a threat to explain to people that they have to be frugal when it comes to their wages and social benefits. At the same time, they are supposed to consume what they have. Companies, on the other hand, are supposed to make ever greater profits because this supposedly creates enough jobs and perhaps ecological solutions. In sum, however, the current state of affairs reveals that it is precisely economics combined with human greed and the desire to constantly maximize profits without regard for long-term consequences that have led to a situation that is ruinous for expectations of a socially just society and sufficiently sustainable development.

We Need an Economic System with a Long View

Most people today live in a capitalist event time and event space with short-term goals, strategies, and desires. The working, economic and living world reflects and contains what is currently given in consumption and possible in relative prosperity. Economically, it has become accepted that profits are increasingly managed by third parties who use the capital profitably for the owners – usually with high personal contributions. A long-term view for the survival and well-being of all is regularly pushed back to short-term profit goals. The wrong incentive already exists in the fact that managers are judged by the level of these profits and rewarded accordingly.

In shareholder value, the corporate social responsibility of capital as an expression of a social market economy that claims to want to serve the common good becomes a secondary matter. This is shown by the fact that there are hardly any persons who can be held responsible and accountable for sustainability damage, such as the destruction of resources, environmental pollution, climate change, or social and economic exploitation. Here, strategies are used that lead to confusing legal forms and clauses of irresponsibility toward a common good that has morally receded into the background. The diesel fraud scandal has shown how, in the central and most important industry of today, leading car producers not only act irresponsibly against people and the environment but then give not even sufficient political and legal liability.[40]

Capitalism is increasingly creating its own norms and rules, with a great deal of invention to find gaps in the national or opportunities in the global. Some of these inventions lead directly to the destruction and exploitation of the planet; some bring exploitation of people as well as corruption.

In the economy today, both the national and the global are strengthened: Globalization of capital secures its liquefied worldwide surplus value and its opportunities to escape regulations and taxes. Nationalization, on the other hand, is used to secure one's own location and to influence politics in order to win over their constituencies with concessions for the lack of alternatives in the economic and distribution system or to conceal damage to people and the environment.

The higher the level of capital, the greater the power to threaten governments with the withdrawal of jobs, the outflow of capital, or with disadvantages on international markets. Influencing governments and influencing state regulations by capital interests, which becomes visible here, is justified by the fact that it enables markets to provide security in their actions and at the same time opportunities for profits.[41] The development of the wealth of a few people shows how much politics thereby favors those who have a lot and disadvantages those who lack everything anyway. As long as the prosperity of broad masses is maintained, this system nevertheless seems invincible. Who should overcome it, when not even the social groups and their respective gains and losses are clearly recognizable anymore, when the imaginary fog of a supposed middle is advertised and played with by politics, when it can no longer be sufficiently understood who bears which responsibility? No matter where people stand socially, they are gladly promised in the imaginary fog before elections that they belong to a relevant majority that is heeded and reinforced by politics. This is precisely why there are only minimal political upheavals in elections in the capitalist system because governments and parties always push toward this imaginary center, where the conservatives suddenly turn green, discover a social vein, and the formerly socialist-oriented bring the low-wage sector into being. But those who economically determine the world remain invisible and yet dominant in all these political moods and strategies for gaining power. Their shortsighted thinking prevents an economic long view.

No Capitalism Is Not a Realistic Solution

The majority of today's political-economic approaches do not see a necessity or a sufficient chance to question capitalism in a radical way because although it is clear to many that the capitalist pursuit of profit has a consistently negative impact on sustainability issues, for today's human imagination and the existing understanding of everyday life, capitalism continues to be seen as the only solution in most cases.[42] Through capitalism alone, the standard of living can be maintained and at the same time, scientific and technological innovations can be found to help the development of further prosperity and progress. From both sides, profit maximization for the rich and super-rich, as well as a rather modest income for the mass of working people, everyone has settled into a limited thinking space in order to maintain prosperity and the prospect of a relatively long life in high security. The people in rich countries have no sufficiently practicable fantasies or promising solutions for an alternative because they have settled into the existing. Anyone who wants to make a fundamental change here immediately makes an enemy of everyone.

The Economic Colonization of the Earth

Rich countries are happy to overlook the raw materials and resources they take, the migration of workers, the consequences of opening up markets, and the globalization of poor countries. Capitalism appears to have no alternative precisely because the rich countries are among the winners in the world. There is a close connection between the temporal development of capitalism and the demand for space in nations, as well as the use of resources in the entire world. On the one hand, spaces are conquered or lost by nations through acts of war, formerly directed toward the acquisition of colonies, now shifted to economic dependence. On the other hand, growing private ownership means that there is hardly any space left that is not someone's private property. The space of the world is not only mapped more and more precisely but also parceled out, legalized, which reduces free use for everyone. This partitioned world functions according to rules; it is owned and so people can be included in it as well as excluded from it. There are rules of ownership according to belonging and denial of entry, fencing, and securitization as basic features of a spatial power that places private law above the claims of the common good. This development is almost always glossed over in the sustainability agenda. How are we to leave a livable future to succeeding generations if it is already so divided within the inherited tenure system that there is little room for new distributions? What does it mean if access to the world's freely usable land is becoming increasingly limited? The consequence of past distribution is clear: When it comes to survival, the poor are always hit the hardest since access to resources remains blocked to them, and they have few possessions. For the particularly poor, this ultimately means displacement and refugee camps in the worst case because they will be the first to suffer from the increasing scarcity of resources, driven to flee, and sent on journeys into the unknown where their human rights play no role whatsoever. Where are they to go when the planet is divided up and sold?[43]

Globalized Value Creation

For centuries, during their industrialization, rich countries simply procured what they needed in raw materials and people from poor countries, especially those of the global south, through colonial policies in order to enable a better economy and way of life for themselves. A paradoxical law of capitalism is that the richer a country is in raw materials, the more likely it is that the majority of the population will live in poverty.

Displacement, flight, and migration are primarily driven by two framework conditions: A tradition of exploitation since colonialism and the effects of human-made climate change and other impacts of lack of sustainability, emanating particularly from the rich countries. It is almost always about capitalist profits, which mainly go to rich countries whose governments, even if they have democratic programs for themselves, hardly deal with the consequences of the pursuit of profit and the greed for raw materials: War and violence are widespread in the struggle for resources, power, and influence; displacement, flight, or migration are the consequences; discrimination and persecution increase in ethnic and religious conflicts; poverty and lack of prospects grow in certain regions or become a permanent problem; land grabbing and trade in raw materials in the exploitation of the countries concerned displace the ancestral population or force them into migration; inequality and repression up to and including civil wars increase.[44] The profit motive is not about introducing democracy everywhere in the world but about squeezing out a maximum for the success of richer countries through profit practices. As long as profits are at stake, even democratic countries do not act consistently against injustice; they are more concerned about undisturbed supply chains. This world of hypocrisy is particularly frustrating for many people who believe in the meaning of democracy.

In the world's most resource-rich regions, which are left empty-handed in globalized value creation, its consequences – such as environmental degradation and climate change – are felt simultaneously earliest and hardest. These countries lack the resources to counter the effects of changing environmental conditions. The Institute for Economics and Peace predicts that up to 31 countries could be uninhabitable by 2050.[45] Storms, floods, or droughts and water scarcity will lead to an increase in social conflicts, wars, and, as a consequence, mass migration. Already today, the inability of, for example, the United States and European Union to manage migration on a relatively small scale shows what a test this will be for rich countries.

How Does Politics Prevent Sustainability?

A turnaround toward sustainability can only be achieved through a new policy.[46] A policy of truth,[47] which is resolutely committed to the implementation of a sustainable way of life, could possibly still avert the approaching catastrophes, first nationally and then globally. But more and more discussions and scientific papers, more and more conferences and target agreements without sufficiently concrete consequences rather testify to the lust for the truth spectacle than to a sufficient will or political possibilities to implement these ideas. How should and can a policy of practiced sustainability be implemented? So far, the assumption seems to prevail in the politics of rich countries that it cannot succeed in adequately solving these challenges without the extensive participation of the private sector.[48] Thus, from the outset, policymakers are subordinating themselves to the economic interests that have been instrumental in causing the crisis. This is also visible in the fact that governments fail especially in making provisions for the future because they make general promises but do not decide on and implement concrete and controllable measures. For example, several G20 heads of state claimed in 2021 to want to give up fossil fuels by around the middle of this century, China wants to become climate-neutral by 2060 and India by 2070, but no one commits to a specific date. The media celebrate the Glasgow climate conference in that all countries agree that there must be climate action, but exactly what the measures will look like and who will be held responsible for them always remains open. A failure is also evident in the fact that the state of affairs is being glossed over by the ruling politicians.

Responsibility Is Shifted to the Individuals

Shifting responsibility to individuals seems to give them freedom and self-determination, but the limited power of individuals means that, above all, policymakers do not want to face the crisis realistically: The lack of sustainability today cannot be regulated individually but only in conjunction with state intervention. In doing so, the measures would first have to be implemented locally in the different nations, which already will be difficult because this will lead to disadvantages for some on the global markets. In the background, the competition between nations always drives the capital to move to where it can maximize best. Thus, governments become susceptible to blackmail. The community of states then is incapable of imposing halfway plausible taxes or regulations because national competition has an effect on the totality of the participating governments through blockades and special paths to one's own profits.

In many cases, governments today have abandoned the idea of making significantly more state investments than in the past in order to serve social equalization, support in cases of disadvantage, the comprehensive development of an equitable education system, free access to the health-care system, and sustainability on a broad scale. They have increasingly focused their responsibility on the economy and its broad promotion. When it comes to social issues, they often transfer responsibility to nonprofit initiatives and increasingly focus on helping people to help themselves. In doing so, they take too little responsibility and even allow rich companies and corporations to influence people to further their own interests. Sponsorship leads to a situation in which interest groups that were already powerful and seeking their own advantage become ever stronger. A media sector determined by private interests then rounds this off.

The Same Old Empty Promises Just Before the Election

The individualization of all problems to be solved on one's own responsibility is often a strategy for politicians to deal with the greatest concern they have: Reelection. The political parties are always anxious about votes, which is dangerous in terms of sustainability because the need for renunciation, a change in lifestyle, and an increase in the price of many things would have to be honestly expressed here. Which party can claim that it has a comprehensive provision in sustainability in mind? Even the Greens, who have a clear focus here, have to compromise on implementation to appear electable. And every concrete demand for higher fuel prices, for example, is immediately exploited populistically by political opponents because they basically still don't care enough about sustainability. Politicians have so far had hardly any assertive concepts to tackle the problem beyond unrealistic promises. That is why the most popular strategy is to present sustainability as an individual problem. Indeed, it is, but not only. For if individuals want to live more sustainably, they will quickly realize that the state must help them comprehensively with framework conditions and regulations, because we need a major, fundamental change of course, the extent of which can only be made by a policy that names things as clearly and unambiguously as they are and then intervenes in a controlling manner.[49]

Up to now, nature and the environment have often been politically pushed back in relation to other issues, and the experiences from the successful economic history and the social distribution struggle of the past very much determine the expectations and solutions in the wishful thinking of majorities.[50] Now sustainability is becoming a challenge that can only be met with large-scale, far-reaching, and politically novel solutions. Politicians are forced to redefine their provision for life in the future. This requires an honest assessment of the situation, which does not continue to rely on waiting but instead decides on concrete measures in controlled time schedules and helps to monitor them. To win majorities for this, new narratives and forms of participation are needed that can bring people along and convince them so that everyone contributes their share to success. This is a precondition to support radical decisions. A majority will only be found if this seems fair and just, if the greatest burdens are not to be borne again by the majorities so that some benefit especially. Politically, there are some cornerstones that need to be considered:

Reduce Economic Inequality Consistently!

First, given the inequality in the world, sustainability can only be managed if the gap between rich and poor is reduced more than before. This inequality exists not only between poor and rich people but also equally between poor and rich countries. There has been a gigantic redistribution of the world's wealth, which will have consequences for later generations. It's time to reverse the trend of a few rich and super-rich getting richer and richer and putting the planet at risk in the process. Policymakers need clear programs of new taxation for more social justice and then also pricing for a lack of sustainability, regulations to promote sustainability, and rewards for sustainable action.

Abolish Growth Myth!

Second, the myth that there is no alternative to an ever-necessary link between growth and sustainability must be abandoned. This myth always leads to a business as usual. And it drives political parties, if they are ecologically oriented, into an already politically presupposed lack of alternatives and adaptation predominantly to existing economic interests. As a result, too many alternative economic forms that are ecological and sustainable are lost from sight. When a party emerges in the ecological movement that wants to advocate sustainability more radically, the theoretical desire for better regulation is shifted into a long march through the institutions, at the latest when the party becomes part of the government. Only when sustainability is demanded by the masses, it seems, can there be a politics of sustainability without perpetual compromise.

Dare to Make Unpleasant Decisions!

Third, a sustainable policy must make a clear commitment: We cannot possess an ultimate truth, but only statements in a struggle for probabilities. In doing so we nevertheless decide in principle for or against a sustainable path. Such a decision will, willy-nilly, involve a series of unpleasant measures, but they are necessary. All people should want to participate in the development of this list of changes and make the decisions for themselves and with others. In a pluralistic society, there will then be other opinions and unsubstantiated claims. The public and many well-meaning people have become accustomed to respecting this and allowing even the greatest foolishness and conspiracy theories under the guise of liberal pluralism. All sustainable people and especially politicians, however, must make it their task to demonstrate as clearly and convincingly as possible the necessities of the sustainable path so that sustainability can be recognized not as a conspiracy but as the only reasonable path to long-term survival.

Sustainability Needs Majorities

Fourth, a policy of sustainability will only succeed if it can win majorities over the long term. At the beginning of this path, this means that politics must, to a greater extent than in the past, give people the opportunity to educate themselves about sustainability without deceptions and illusions. Sustainability is a national, as well as an international, educational task that must be prioritized in the education system, which must gain greater influence in the media, and that must – this will be a particularly difficult claim – expose as untrustworthy the many media and lobbying outlets influenced by profit interests that downplay sustainability and discredit the sustainable path.

Policymakers Must Strengthen Scientific Freedom and Freedom of Expression

The four points can only be achieved if the level of social enlightenment changes.[51] Democracy should not be confused with everyone being able to say anything without being questioned. Hate should not be allowed to spread in anonymity without scrutiny and punishment just because it seems democratic, even though it is inhumane. It is time to socially regain a minimum of scientificity and to publicly name as wrong what is taken out of the air or only serves one-sided interests. The sciences should not be forced to orient their research predominantly to economic interests and contract research. Universities must become free from the influence of private capital and be able to conduct basic research with greater breadth and independence.[52] The media should no longer simply pass on everything that drives up circulation but should be able to choose to be scientifically based or to comment critically on what often remains superficial as sensationalism. In many media, there is a preselection that is presented as a diversity of opinions, but in reality, it represents manipulated opinions in favor of certain interests. Politically, therefore, it should be an important goal to place an emphasis on education, on seeing through such processes, and on immunizing people against them through scientific education. At the same time, there is a need to strengthen the independence of the media through state-funded independent journalism and media, which should be expanded.

Today, the attack on scientific freedom and freedom of opinion also takes place through consumption and digital strategies, which, despite all the differences in the goods and offers, are designed to be synchronized in virtual capitalism.[53] In many countries, this is also used politically. In China and other despotic systems, total surveillance prevails.

Any restriction on freedom of expression is dangerous for democracies, but freedom of expression can also be exploited: For manipulation, misdirection, and conspiracy, used to spread untruths or to push through certain commercial interests. As long as people are so vulnerable to propaganda and opinion-making, as long as opinion and knowledge can only be distinguished when everyone receives a better education and does not allow themselves to be dominated by selective interests, as long as the common good does not once again come more to the fore, there is a need for an actively democratic and sustainable increase in accountability in all places of science and opinion-forming that recovers critical thinking and opens up an age of sustainable enlightenment for as many as possible.

Notes

1 Humanity has developed a materialism in behavior, which is reflected in consumption, cf., e.g., Bauman, Z. (2007): *Consuming Life*. Cambridge: Polity Press; Kasser, T. (2002): *The High Price of Materialism*. Cambridge, MA: MIT Press.

2 One of the first introductions to the topic offers Marcuse, H. (1964): One-Dimensional Man: Studies in the Ideology of Advanced Industrial Society. https://www.marcuse.org/herbert/pubs/64onedim/odmcontents.html

3 Referring back to Hobbes, Bauman discusses the extent to which this corresponds to a struggle of all against all. See Bauman, Z. (2017): *Retrotopia*. Cambridge: Polity. At the same time, it raises the question of what moral boundaries still apply here: Bauman, Z. (2008): *Does Ethics Have a Chance in a World of Consumers?* Cambridge: Harvard University Press.

4 This is particularly illustrated by Klein, N. (2008): *The Shock Doctrine. The Rise of Desaster Capitalism*. New York: Metropolitan Books; Klein, N. (2015): *This Changes Everything*. London: Penguin.

5 Cf. Bauman, Z. (2004): *Wasted Lives. Modernity and Its Outcasts.* Cambridge: Polity Press.

6 The work of Zygmunt Bauman in particular can help to define this new starting position more precisely, e.g., Bauman, Z. (1993): *Modernity and Ambivalence.* Cambridge and Oxford: Polity Press; Bauman, Z. (1995): *Life in Fragments: Essays in Postmodern Morality.* Cambridge, MA: Basil Blackwell; Bauman, Z. (1997): *Postmodernity and its Discontents.* New York: New York University Press; Bauman, Z. (2000): *Liquid Modernity.* Cambridge: Polity Press.

7 Some critical aspects that constitute a collapse of societies are discussed in Diamond, J. (2005): *Collapse: How Societies Choose to Fail or Succeed.* London: Penguin.

8 Cf. Machiavelli, N. (1961): *The Prince.* London: Penguin.

9 It is a materialistic world, see Miller, D. (1987): *Material Culture and Mass Consumption.* Oxford: Blackwell; Miller, D. (Hg.) (2005): *Materiality.* Durham, NC: Duke University Press.

10 The extent to which this distribution brings democracy itself to its end is discussed by Crouch, C. (2004): *Post–Democracy.* Cambridge and Oxford: Polity; Crouch, C. (2011): *The Strange Non–death of Neo–liberalism.* Cambridge and Oxford: Polity; Crouch, C. (2016): The March Towards Post–Democracy, Ten Years On. *The Political Quarterly*, 87(1), January–March 2016.

11 Cf. Piketty, T. (2014): *Capital in the Twenty–First Century.* Cambridge and London: Harvard University Press. More specific: Alvaredo, F., Chancel, L., Piketty, T., Saez, E., & Zucman, G. (2017): *World Inequality Report 2018.* Paris: World Inequality Lab.

12 There are well-founded analyses of what could be done about inequality, but policymakers have not yet followed such analyses. Cf. Atkinson, A. B. (2015): *Inequality: What Can Be Done?* Cambridge and London: Harvard University Press.

13 A classic model of this way of thinking can be found here Smith, A. (1976 [1776]): *An Inquiry into the Nature and Causes of the Wealth of Nations.* Oxford: Oxford University Press. New forms of the development are discussed here: Stiglitz, J. (2006): *Making Globalization Work.* London: W.W. Norton & Company.

14 Examples can be found in Kasser, T. & Ryan, R. M. (1993): A Dark Side of the American Dream: Correlates of Financial Success as a Central Life Aspiration. *Journal of Personal and Social Psychology*, 65, 410–422; Kasser, T., Ryan, R. M., Couchman, C. E. & Sheldon, K. M. (2003): Materialistic Values: Their Causes and Consequences. In T. Kasser & A. D. Kanner (Eds.), *Psychology and Consumer Culture. The Struggle for a Good Life in a Materialistic World (11–29).* Washington, DC: American Psychological Association.

15 See   https://www.oxfam.org/en/press-releases/carbon-emissions-richest-1-percent-more-double-emissions-poorest-half-humanity

16 See, e.g., Galvin, R. & Sunikka-Blank, M. (2018): Economic Inequality and Household Energy Consumption in High-Income Countries: A Challenge for Social Science Based Energy Research. *Ecological Economics*, 153, 78–88.

17 See, e.g., Foer, J. S. (2019): *We are the Weather.* New York: Farar, Strauss & Giroux.

18 And this is always connected to inequality. See, e.g., https://www.oecd.org/
competition/inequality-a-hidden-cost-of-market-power.htm

19 Actual data can be found here: https://earthobservatory.nasa.gov/
global-maps/MOD14A1_M_FIRE

20 The roots of the destruction of the Amazon go back a long time and lie
in capitalism; see, e.g., Bunker, S. (1985): *Underdeveloping the Amazon:
Extraction, Unequal Exchange, and the Failure of the Modern State.*
Chicago: University of Chicago Press.

21 Barriers to behavior change are discussed extensively by Gifford, R. (2011):
The Dragons of Inaction. Psychological Barriers That Limit Climate
Change Mitigation and Adaptation. *American Psychologist. American
Psychological Association*, May–June 2011, 66(4), 290–302; Gifford, R. et
al. (2009): Temporal Pessimism and Spatial Optimism in Environmental
Assessments. An 18–Nation Study. *Journal of Environmental Psychology*,
29, 1–12; Gifford, R., Kormos, C., & McIntyre, A. (2011): *Behavioral
Dimensions of Climate Change: Drivers, Responses, Barriers, and
Interventions: WIREs Clim Change* 2011, John Wiley & Sons; Gifford, R.
& Nilsson, A. (2014): Personal and Social Factors That Influence Pro–envi-
ronmental Concern and Behaviour. *International Journal of Psychology*,
49, 141–157. See also Leviston, C. & Uren, H. V. (2020): Overestimating
One's "Green" Behavior: Better–Than–Average Bias May Function to
Reduce Perceived Personal Threat from Climate Change. *Journal of Social
Issues*, 76(1), 70–85.

22 This agenda must be guided by the scientific research data on sustainability and not by the interests of the business lobby; cf., e.g., endnote 13.

23 Cf. Norgaard, K. M. (2011): *Living in Denial. Climate Change, Emotions,
and Everyday Life.* Cambridge: MIT Press; Norgaard, K.M. (2019): Making
Sense of the Spectrum of Climate Denial. *Critical Policy Studies*, 13, 437–441.

24 The propaganda model of such influence has been analyzed above all
by Chomsky; see, e.g., Chomsky, N. (1989): *Necessary Illusions. Thought
Control in Democratic Societies*. London: Pluto Press; Chomsky, N. &
Herman, E. S. (1994): *Manufacturing Consent. The Political Economy of
the Mass Media*. London: Vintage; Herman, E. S. & Chomsky, N. (2006):
Manufacturing Consent. The Political Economy of the Mass Media. New
York: Pantheon.

25 See, e.g., Oreskes, N. & Conway, E. (2010): *Merchants of Doubt: How a
Handful of Scientists Obscured the Truth from Tobacco Smoke to Global
Warming*. New York: Bloomsbury Press.

26 Overviews of empirical meta-analyses in research show very clearly how
much wishful thinking determines the formation of opinion in the sus-
tainability sector; see, e.g., Hines, J., Hungerford, H. R., & Tomera, A.
N. (1986–1987): Analysis and Synthesis of Research on Responsible
Environmental Behavior. A Meta–Analysis. *Journal of Environmental
Education*, 18(2), 1–8; Bamberg, S., & Moser, G. (2007): Twenty years after
Hines, Hungerford, and Tomera. A New Meta–Analysis of Psycho–Social
Determinants of Pro–Environmental Behavior. *Journal of Environmental
Psychology*, 27, 14–25.

27 Critical in terms of desired and actual behavior, see Kormos, C. & Gifford,
R. (2014): The validity of self–report measures of proenvironmental behavior. A meta–analytic review. *Journal of Environmental Psychology*, 40,

December 2014, 359–371; Webb, T. L. & Sheeran, P. (2006): Does Changing Behavioral Intentions Engender Behavior Change? A Meta–Analysis of the Experimental Evidence. *Psychological Bulletin*, 132(2), 249–268.

28 Cf., e.g., Stern, N. (2006): *The Economics of Climate Change*. Cambridge: Cambridge University Press; Stern, N. (2016): *Why Are We Waiting? The Logic, Urgency, and Promise of Tackling Climate Change*. Cambridge: The MIT Press.

29 Cf., e.g., Neal, L. & Williamson, J. (Eds.) (2014): *The Cambridge History of Capitalism. (2 Bde.)* Cambridge.

30 See, e.g., Robson, W. A. (2015): *The Wellfare Society*. London: Routledge.

31 See, e.g., Latouche, S. (2009): *Farewell to Growth*. Cambridge: Polity Press.

32 See, e.g., Jackson, T. (2009): *Prosperity Without Growth: Economics for a finite Planet*. London: Earthscan.

33 Like Schumacher, E. F. (1973): *Small Is Beautiful. Economics as if People Mattered*. New York: Harper and Row.

34 See, e.g., Webb, J. (2012): Climate Change and Society. The Chimera of Behaviour Change Technologies. *Sociology*, 46(1) (Sage, February 2012), 109–125.

35 Cf. Foster, J. B. (1999): Marx's Theory of Metabolic Rift: Classical Foundations for Environmental Sociology. *American Journal of Sociology*, 105(2), 366–405; Foster, J. B., Clark, B., & York, R. (2010): *The Ecological Rift. Capitalism's War on the Earth*. New York: Monthly Review Press.

36 On recent economic theories of how surplus values are formed, see esp. Bourdieu, P. (1986) The Forms of Capital. In: J. Richardson (Hg.) *Handbook of Theory and Research for the Sociology of Education* (New York, Greenwood), 241–258; Reich, K. (2018): *Surplus Values. A Theory of Forms of Capital for the Twenty–First Century*. Cologne: University of Cologne. http://www.uni–koeln.de/hf/konstrukt/english/surplus_value/index.html

37 Cf., e.g., Stiglitz, J. (2010): *Freefall: America, Free Markets, and the Sinking of the World Eco*. London: W.W. Norton & Company.

38 It is a world in pieces: Geertz, C. (2000): The World in Pieces. Culture and Politics at the End of the Century. In: *Available Light: Anthropological Reflections on Philosophical Topics*. Princeton, NJ: Princeton University Press, 218–263.

39 Cf. Graeber, D. (2011): *Debt: The first 5.000 Years*. Brooklyn, NY: Melville House.

40 On the relationship between capitalism and fraud cf. Galbraith, J. K. (2004): *The Economics of Innocent Fraud: Truth for Our Time*. New York: Houghton Mifflin

41 From the numerous analyses in this field, see in particular Crouch in endnote 10; Blühdorn, I. (2014): Post–Ecologist Governmentality. Post–Democracy, Post–Politics and the Politics of Unsustainability. In: Swyngedouw, E. & Wilson, J. (Eds.) (2014): *The Post–Political and its Discontents*. Edinburgh: Edinburgh University Press; Blühdorn, I. (2015): *Post–Ecologist Politics*. London and New York: Routledge.

42 See, e.g., Bowerman, T. (2014): How Much Is Too Much? A Public Opinion Research Perspective. *Sustainability: Science, Practice and Policy*, 10(1), 14–28.

43 See, e.g., Sassen, S. (2014): *Expulsions. Brutality and Complexity in the Global Economy*. Cambridge and London: The Belknap Press of Harvard University Press; Sassen, S. (2008): *Territory, Authority, Rights*. Princeton and Oxford: Princeton University Press.

44 See, e.g., Mignolo, W. (2011): *The Darker Side of Western Modernity. Global Futures, Decolonial Options.* Durham and London: Duke University Press.

45 Cf. https://www.economicsandpeace.org/

46 Cf, e.g., in general Giddens, A. (2011): *The Politics of Climate Change.* Cambridge: Polity Press; with a focus on the relationship between nature and capitalization Moore, J. W. (Ed.) (2016): *Anthropocene or Capitalocene? Nature, History, and the Crisis of Capitalism.* Oakland, CA: PM Press; from a radical position that separates human history in its continuity from the actions that seem to be naturally necessary (a position I don't completely share because from a human point of view, there is no nature per se): Latour, B. (2017): *Facing Gaia. Eight Lectures on the New Climatic Regime.* Cambridge: Polity; and Latour, B. (2018): *Down to Earth. Politics in the New Climate Regime.* Cambridge, UK: Polity.

47 Truth here understood in the sense of scientific probability. Since John Dewey, it should be self-evident to understand truth as an expression of human knowledge of action; cf., for instance, Garrison, J., Neubert, S., & Reich, K. (2012): *John Dewey's Philosophy of Education – An Introduction and Recontextualization for Our Times.* New York: Palgrave Macmillan; Garrison, J., Neubert, S., & Reich, K. (2016): *Democracy and Education Reconsidered. 100 Years after Dewey.* London/New York: Routledge.

48 Some counter-designs can be found – e.g., in Nelson, A. & Timmerman, F. (Eds.) (2011): *Life Without Money. Building Fair and Sustainable Economies.* London: Pluto Press.

49 A study that comprehensively addresses and analyzes all these aspects is Hornborg, A. (2019): *Nature, Society, and Justice in the Anthropocene.* Cambridge and New York: Cambridge University Press.

50 Confer, for example, to empirical studies like Capstick, S., Whitmarsh, L., Poortinga, W., Pidgeon, N., & Upham, P. (2014): International Trends in Public Perceptions of Climate Change over the Past Quarter Century. *WIRES Climate Change*, 6, 35–61; Pelletier, L. G., Dion, S., Tuson, K., & Green–Demers, I. (1999): Why Do People Fail to Adopt Environmental Protective Behaviors? Toward a Taxonomy of Environmental Amotivation. *Journal of Applied Social Psychology*, 29, 12, 2481–2504; Kousky, C., Rostapshova, O., Toman, M., & Zeckhauser, R. (2009): Responding to Threats of Climate Change Mega–Catastrophes. HKS Faculty Research Working Paper Series, RWP10–008, November 2009, John F. *Kennedy School of Government*, Harvard University; Leiserowitz, A. (2007): *Public Perception, Opinion and Understanding of Climate Change. Current Patterns, Trends and Limitations.* New York: United Nations Development Programme; Frantz, C. M. & Mayer, F. S. (2009): The Emergency of Climate Change: Why Are We Failing to Take Action? *Analyses of Social Issues and Public Policy*, 9(1), 205–222; Sandvik, H. (2008): Public Concern Over Global Warming Correlates Negatively with National Wealth. *Climatic Change*, 90(3), 333–341.

51 Enlightenment is endangered in many ways today. People everywhere are manipulated for commercial interests. See, e.g., Akerlof, G. A. & Shiller, R– J. (2015): *Phishing for Phools. The Economics of Manipulation and Deception.* Princeton: Princeton University Press. See also endnote 24.

52 Cf., e.g., Resnik, D. (2007): *The Price of Truth. How Money Affects the Norms of Science*. Oxford: Oxford University Press; Donoghue, F. (2008): *The Last Professors. The Corporate University and the Fate of the Humanities*. New York: Fordham.
53 Cf. Zuboff, S. (2015): Big Other: Surveillance Capitalism and the Prospects of an Information Civilization. *Journal of Information Technology*, 30, 75–89; Zuboff, S. (2019): *The Age of Surveillance Capitalism: The Fight for a Human Future at the New Frontier of Power*. New York: PublicAffairs.

3 Consequences

What Should We Do?

Develop Your Own Sustainable Attitude!

Sustainability begins with the individual; each and every one of us is called upon to live more sustainably. First and foremost, every human being strives for his or her own survival, but at the same time, he or she is also committed to his or her living environment, which makes this life possible and sustains it in the first place. Those who want to participate in this world in an enlightened way must inform and educate themselves about it and, in particular, must step out of sustainable immaturity. Individually, it is a matter of acquiring sustainable knowledge and developing an attitude based on it, which exercises environmentally compatible behavior, instead of despairing among all the conflicting ideas and ultimately giving up. People become more successful at this when they learn to identify where and how their actions are good or harmful to the environment and can thus clearly name what they can concretely change in their everyday lives and beyond.

Movies Show Us Our Fears

But today, the challenges of sustainability – e.g., climate change – are hardly ever experienced directly and immediately for all. Even after a brief exposure to the consequences of a lack of sustainability, it becomes clear that we are heading toward a situation where people might show their ugly sides in the struggle for survival. But recognizing this is currently more a question of education, a question of how far there is sufficient predictive power about the consequences in each individual. Especially in disaster movies, humanity is shown what could happen in the worst-case scenario owing to weapons of mass destruction, climate change, resource depletion, increasing greed on

DOI: 10.4324/9781003276449-3

one side, and injustice on the other.[1] This makes sense to us when it happens personified and a clear distinction is made between good and evil because then it is not about boring abstract models of science. At the same time, however, we are becoming more and more numbed by media dramatizations, often find it difficult to distinguish between reality and virtuality, and can hardly assess scientifically what is actually coming our way. Sure, biodiversity is declining. But aren't insects a nuisance anyway? And at what point does species extinction become a threat to humans? Well, bacterial germs are becoming increasingly resistant and viruses are spreading worldwide, but when will the first mass extinction begin? When will we be part of it? And the temperature? The 1-degree target has remained pure fantasy; the 1.5-degree target is currently cracked; 2 degrees is unstoppable anyway. In the end, we will have to talk about many more degrees. But what does the increase mean in concrete terms? Sea levels are rising, but what does that mean to me here, in this place, on what day?

We cannot let our image be determined predominantly by fiction; we have to turn to the facts in the development of our own sustainable attitude, everyone is called upon to do so!

Consumption and Renunciation

Consumption determines our lives. We work to acquire food and consumer goods. The paying consumer rules the world – and this world itself, its biodiversity, its balanced ecology, and the climate that enables all living beings to live at all, has no fixed seat in this government. What matters more so far are the wishful, advertised truths: Most people want to expand and embellish their living space, take trips all over the world, and keep increasing or refining their needs for mobility, food, and pleasure. Consumption is so successful as a guiding principle of individualization because it can be tied to desires and their satisfactions. A change to sustainability as a goal in life is much more difficult to achieve because here less is necessary, which for the individual acts like a punishment, a limitation, and a curtailment of possibilities, as long as primarily consumption documents a successful life.

We have to change! The change aims at a more sustainable world in which it is possible for everyone to still lead a fulfilled life but in which the world itself, nature, and the environment, which is the habitat of all of us, gain priority. If for this change, renunciation in consumption and an overcoming of affluence are necessary, then this will be, in the long run, sustainable progress that serves survival.

Prioritize the Ecological Issue!

The desire for social justice and thus social sustainability is an ongoing issue in capitalism because the focus on profit and ownership by too many leads inevitably to more inequality. Although the improvements won by social movements for the disadvantaged have produced important changes in the well-being of many, today these issues must be connected with the ecological question. We have to prioritize the fight for sustainability because there is not much time left to counter the downward trends: Greenhouse gases are rising relentlessly, and it will take centuries to reduce them. So we have to set a completely new bar on these issues, one that is initially inconceivable to human life and the time in which we usually calculate. Short-term thinking has led us to where we are today and must be replaced by one that also considers long-term consequences.[2] If, for example, today nuclear power is supposed to help achieve the CO_2 targets in the short term, we have to consider the radioactively contaminated tanks in Fukushima that are to be discharged into the sea. Once again, shortsighted savings are being made, and posterity will be left with a problem for which it will despise us. Today, it can no longer be primarily a matter of wishes, but the boundaries of Earth must be brought to the fore. With regard to climate change and its consequences, it makes little sense to invoke commodity-money relations now for nature and the solution of sustainability issues, because the biophysical world is not about market laws and social constructions, not about how unequal or equal the exchange between nature, raw materials, resources, and money is. Rather, already on an individual level, we must learn to think more strongly from nature again, to be gentle, protective, and preserving.[3] We should not only appreciate the beautiful sight of nature and the wonders of life in quiet moments but also internalize the desire to preserve the natural, the beauties of nature, and life on the planet in such a way that contravention is experienced with shame, doubt, or disgust. Here lies the beginning of individual sustainability!

Everyone Must Take Responsibility for the Common Good!

The state has shifted a large part of its responsibility for provision to individuals, who are supposed to take care of their own well-being in the struggle of all against all. The concern for oneself grows in isolation, it is accompanied by concepts of self-management, the increase of self-worth, self-confidence in the competitive struggle, self-confidence in one's own possibilities, and constant self-optimization.

In education and media, all these desires are served with a diversity of perspectives because in neoliberal economics and politics, borders are opened, migration of labor is necessary, differences of wealth with social gradient are desired. Within all this diversity, the common good has been deferred. Now, in terms of sustainability, it suddenly becomes important again, but today it has become incomprehensible to many people. Why should I take care of my fellow citizen if she or he is also my competitor? Why should I recycle waste when others simply throw it away? Why should I bear more environmental costs than others who, on the other hand, continue to live in luxury?

People today are looking above all for solutions for themselves, even if these can usually only be effective in the short term. The detachment from fixed orders and traditional communities has made many personal freedoms possible, but at the same time, it has also weakened the sense of obligation to the community and a sense of belonging to nature. The question of the future of the world, however, depends on the common good; it is lost if the individual's only concern is to lead his or her life free of responsibilities and in as much prosperity as is possible. Through individualization, humanity has been strongly influenced to avoid conflict, but in sustainability, it is precisely resistance and work on oneself and others that are needed. The sense of responsibility toward future generations has steadily decreased, especially in rich countries, which is the background for today's lack of sustainability.[4] So far, it leaves the perpetrators of the great damages unscathed because consumption lures too many to want to participate in an individualized way until the last hour.

Against the backdrop of individualization, the sustainability literature is riddled with advisers of individual behavioral change on a small scale. In shopping for fairly produced food, in determining its effect on nature and the environment, in disposing of leftovers and garbage. This change alone can quickly become overwhelming because supply chains remain opaque, the components of consumer goods are unclear, and an estimate of the impact on greenhouse gas production or other harms seems difficult to assess on an individual basis. The sustainable world is too complicated to understand and regulate everything on one's own.[5] Nevertheless, it is necessary to have one's own view, to build up knowledge, an attitude that understands sustainability as a problem and a central challenge for one's own future, and to develop a sustainable attitude that guides one's own actions. In doing so, an exclusively egoistic view must be overcome because the common good of an ecologically better-balanced world can only be achieved or fought for together with others.

Fear Drives People to Change!

Individual knowledge about sustainability is an important starting point. Schools play a central role in this. Unfortunately, however, sustainability forms only a small part of the current curriculum, which also mostly consists of mere book knowledge. If learners find facts about the greenhouse effect on an assignment sheet and memorize them as knowledge alongside other content, this is unlikely to generate sufficient behavior change.[6] Many studies in behavioral research show that people can derive knowledge from insight but hardly change their behavior.[7] In this respect, individual sustainability always includes fears of a threatened future. Only when we actively live more sustainably will these fears be able to transform into manageable concerns.[8] Unfortunately, there are still very many nonsustainable people who first need disasters before they even develop such fears and are thus motivated to act. Even if it would not be good to constantly fuel the fears, it would be fatal if they are merely repressed and not dealt with. Lack of sustainability in its many aspects gives rise to justified fears! It is precisely these fears that can and should be the impetus for us to face the challenge more strongly.

At the same time, there are also sustainable people who fall into despair because of fear or worry, because they realize again and again how little they can really achieve, they despair because of slowness or insufficient results.[9] The fight for sustainability does not perform quick miracles, it is arduous, and the sustainable must keep reminding themselves that they can fail even in small matters if their ideals become too big and can no longer be reconciled with reality. The same is true for the sustainable: The journey is more than the destination in the short run, and compromises are always demanded along the way. At the same time, however, only joining together in sustainable groups can protect the individual from letting lazy compromises take over.

Overcoming the Repression of the Crisis!

The sustainability crisis is perfect for denial because while we know about it and hear about it every day, its impacts are often ambiguous or even far away, making it easy to ignore. It is precisely the slowness of events to occur and their disparate impacts in the world that make it so easy to put any action into perspective: "What I do won't change anything anyway, and things don't look that bad around us." Our judgments are usually based on what we have perceived recently.[10] But the climate is slowly changing. We are not always there when resources are wasted. We don't notice their absence until they are already gone. The real catastrophe seems to be far in the future, so a few hot summers are not enough to really worry us. We have air conditioning; we have sufficient wealth to adapt to extreme weather events; we can obtain supplies from global markets when our own agriculture or animal husbandry fails. We learn a lot about the negative numbers we measure – for example, in CO_2 emissions year after year with rising curves – but in everyday life, it all still remains rather abstract. We still have too few concrete ideas of what this will mean for us in the future. And since we have been brought up to think in the short term anyway, it is easy to ignore it because the current consumer society builds its business model precisely on such short-termism and shortsightedness.[11]

A Sustainable Art of Living

Our judgments are influenced by ideological and social affiliations and by our own experiences of our achieved prosperity, which we want to classify and understand against the background of our affiliations and desires. Even in the case of environmental catastrophes that directly affect people, it usually seems easier to explain them as coincidence and fate than to assume probabilities that everyone should be intensively concerned about. Many always worry more about the present but less about a future that is still in the distance. If we think of our own mortality, even this is still very far away, even for the oldest among us it seems to be far in the future. The more unclear the risks are, the riskier we want to live.[12] This can only be counteracted by shock experiences[13] or an education[14] that explains and presents the probable processes so clearly that we can no longer close our eyes. We need a policy that shows that collective action can very well bring about change. And we need to learn to look more critically at our desired world.

Even if we acquire a knowledge of sustainability, we run the risk of stopping after the first steps. What makes us hesitate? We ourselves always want to be treated fairly in terms of our interests and concerns, our needs, and our prosperity, but how fair this is to others and how damaging it is to the planet is less likely to occur to us. It always remains possible to pretend to be ecologically committed and yet live in luxury, to continue to collect air miles in order to be able to fly even more, or to speed along the highway in an SUV – best without a speed limit – in order to enjoy mobility and freedom. Anyone who throws trash on the street can be immediately identified and held accountable, but CO_2 emissions remain hidden in plain sight. And this is where social evaluation comes into play: We don't seem to have to be ashamed of such behavior because those who drive Porsches instead of bicycles are considered successful, because practicing nonsustainability is still met with envy rather than contempt. This is a decisive reason why many people – after taking the first steps toward a sustainable attitude – begin to have doubts because it contradicts the values of our society and perhaps also their own desires.

In a world where everything is measured exactly in euros and dollars, it is difficult to deal with relations, exponential assumptions, probable statements. These difficulties can cause us to turn away and immediately give up everything. But we can also decide to stand up and develop our own sustainable attitude that is not satisfied with what seems predetermined. We can decide not to remain in fear but to cast off despondency and be curious about what lies behind and what can be done. We can take our own destiny into our own hands and at the same time take a critical and inquiring look at the world. The current crisis, however, is a challenge that is no longer just about individual survival or more fairness in social distribution but about the survival of humanity as a whole.

Up to now, it has been considered an art of living if our life is filled with individual satisfaction, which enables us not to lose ourselves in all the hectic and demands of work, performance, and lifestyle, not to end up in stress, burnout, or depression. Above all, art, literature, aesthetics, movement, and the other manifold sides of self-realization seem to help to creatively unfold one's own ego and to find a balance between ego and world.[15] If the individual is to find his or her sustainability gratifying, then an alternative, sustainable art of living is needed that combines creative self-realization with the opportunities of social relationships in a protected environment. In this process, limits and renunciation, a sustainable drive for action, and thinking out of the previous ego box in the direction of the common good become cornerstones of a change that can open up a new satisfaction. The first road in such an art of living will have to fight with many resistances; it will meet many opponents against whom it has to assert itself. It will turn against the deniers, the forgetful, or the ignorant who only allow their world view in seeking their advantages. It is high time that the sustainable people of the world refute the fairy tales of ever-increasing prosperity and unrestrained growth with the same quality of life, while not losing their own joy and fun in the argument. A sustainable art of living reveals a new dimension of the sustainable-social intelligence of human beings, which can be more attractive than merely joining the stream of indifference and acquiring more and more consumer goods!

Look for Incentives That Continuously Strengthen Your Sustainable Self-Efficacy!

Once you have taken the first steps toward a sustainable attitude, a new challenge awaits you: The leap from insight to self-efficacious action, which controls one's own sustainability and gives it impulses to do more. If a sustainable attitude is present, imperfect perhaps, but knowledge and insight are given, and there is a desire to make a difference, the beginning is set, but the goal is still a long way off. What is needed now to continue sustainable behavior is the experience of self-efficacy. This means the experience that one's own actions are actually successful, that the sustainable attitude leads to demonstrably more sustainability.[16] This can create a cycle of self-reinforcement in which the attitude is rewarded by the resulting action outcomes.[17] Miracles do not have to happen immediately, but at least small successes with perspective are helpful. Only if this can succeed will sustainable people follow their paths and be role models for others.

Shift Self-Efficacy from Consumption to Greater Sustainability

Today, we experience ourselves as self-effective, above all as consumers. Because through consumer goods, we can reward ourselves well and thus achieve quick successes. To this end, we also use social media with productions of small differences, triviality, and the trivial, which we send around the world as images, text messages, sound, and video to draw attention to ourselves. Our dreams are thereby constantly compared with others; it is a world of continuous self-reflection that makes us feel like being there. We could now replace this triviality with a decision for sustainability and turn it into an aspiration, into a sustainable belonging: The goal could be to henceforth give the world an ecological value, to proclaim and post it everywhere, to multiply and advertise it, to envision a successful world in ecological balance. Or to critically discuss its absence. Conversations about it could be the reason for action: For finding and removing trash locally, for educating others about the dimensions of sustainability, for researching water and air quality locally, for pointing out gaps in regulations and laws. If we spent half as much energy in such commitment to sustainability as we do on shopping, we would already have turned a corner. If we can avoid waste, wear textiles differently and longer, value minimalism,[18] zero waste,[19] and vegetarian or vegan diets, the images and messages about them might fill our social media, which we send around the world and which our social groups acknowledge. Then we will notice that – a little at first, then more and more – a shift in values is taking place: It is now considered when our world does not go out as soon as internet access fails, or we do not have the latest smartphone model; we suddenly appreciate it again when face-to-face communication comes back. We are no longer so preoccupied with consumption that there is no time left for sustainability. Nature and the environment play a greater role again, as do existential questions that deal with what is really necessary for survival instead of the plethora of trivial differences in consumption or mere luxury. Then it would be possible to recognize that the struggle for mundane consumption has taken up too much precious life time, too much space that could be filled with more important things. What has been lost in relationships, friendships, and love, we could win back. We should enjoy it again beyond bargain hunting, mere leisure consumption, and the like. Sustainable people are looking for a nature without the leisure industry. They want to develop a new social and ecological intelligence that finds its joy and fun in the freedom of creativity beyond the shackles of material status.

Self-Efficacy in Risk Prevention

People who spend a lot of money on prevention and precautions against storms and other catastrophes can only experience themselves as successful and self-effective if the invested costs – for example, for insurances or expensive and protected residential buildings – can be put into a realistic relation to an imminent loss. The less likely this loss appears in one's own place of residence or is portrayed in public, the media, and politics, the less likely preventive behavior will be.[20] Despite all the risks, people want above all to experience themselves as self-efficacious. Therefore, it is helpful if, overall, for all sustainable efforts, such experiences are visualized in a simple, vivid way on a daily basis: Determine your own footprint and visualize when you have made progress in reducing it. Show how you're making gains in overcoming waste, better heating, and composting. Don't look for the big miracles but the small impacts that will become miracles when many others do the same. Look for tools, apps, and blogs to help you do this. Find out the pollutant content, the amount of microplastic, pollution, and poison in all your consumer goods. Rejoice with others that you are regaining decision criteria to decide for or against something. Use the internet and forums to inform yourself, to exchange ideas, to counterbalance where social regulation has failed so far. It is self-effective if you gain criteria about the sustainable value of every good in your life.

Nudge for the Good

With the capitalistic markets, humanity has entered an age of comprehensive influence, which is characterized by advertising, wishful thinking, as well as ignorance of resulting consequences for the environment. In the human sciences, the view has spread that biological evolution has equipped humans with two perceptual systems to ensure their survival[21]:

One system is nonlinguistic, fast, and experiential, acting and reacting to a high degree emotionally, intuitively, and often following gut feelings and holistic perceptions. This corresponds to human intentions, which are mixed with wishes and projections for a successful life and need an open perception of possible chances in all situations connected with will and drive. This system is especially emotionally appealed to by the advertising industry of the consumer society.

The other system is more rational, cool, slow, and distant. Will and drive are put here on the thought test and in the execution on the success test, provided that patience, time, perseverance, and enough energy are present. This system is gladly manipulated by persuasion, promises, and embellished representations from the outside.

If we look at both systems, then human behavior is usually easier to influence than we ourselves would like to believe possible. People can be nudged in many ways and often are manipulated hereby.[22] The economy relies with all its might on such influence through its advertising. In capitalism, the goal of the nudge is hidden, just as the originators remain invisible. The nudged should rather assume that they have motivated themselves because they believe that they lack the nudged product and thus think that they absolutely need it.

Surveys show that when people are asked about smoking, energy, water consumption, saving for old age, or their sustainability, they prefer the rational system 2 to retain more control, even though system 1 usually produces higher effects for behavior change. In today's advertising in all fields of influencing, an elaborate manipulation machine has emerged that can manipulate people with ease. Numerous studies of media theory prove this development. Nudges are used everywhere to influence people because people will only fundamentally change their behavior if their emotions, their desires, and their fears are also addressed. Through rational arguments alone, they can understand things and consider them to be right, but their actions very rarely change as a result. In relation to such strategies, it is therefore first of all central to become aware of how impressionable we are and whose interests become visible when we look at concrete nudges. The basic question is, Do we want to be influenced to buy or do something that, on reflection, we basically don't want? Or do we want to influence and incentivize ourselves to change a behavior, to positively incentivize ourselves for purposes worth living for? In both ways, it is obvious that our behavior today is strongly influenced via nudges. That's why billions are poured into advertising. Unfortunately, significantly less gets to where it's about strengthening the common good. Advertisements for sustainable ideas, products, and behaviors are competing with a commercial market that uses all means of influence and can only survive against it if they use the same tools to fight for a better world. Since such advertising then does not set profit as its goal, it can, however, always reveal and make visible the strategies of influence. For example, in the eco-market, there is a sign saying, "We have placed this at your eye level so that you can find and buy this product more easily! We consider it sustainable for the following reasons: …!" Such honesty is needed in advertising for more sustainability to keep the sustainable persuasion transparent. Since the sustainable do not have advertising billions, it takes a high level of commitment and creative ideas to develop a sustainable nudge culture.

Sustainability Needs a Compelling Narrative

Changing people's behavior is easier if they can make themselves believe the narrative of the lack of sustainability, if they learn to look and acknowledge that they are facing an enormous threat. This narrative must appeal to systems 1 and 2 at the same time. But how can we make more room for such narratives in our daily lives – or rather, alongside our hectic daily lives? How can we unfold sufficient forces to enlighten ourselves about ourselves?

It is good to start with ourselves and ask to what extent we contribute to our ecological world and its outcome (use internet research to find tools for measurement):

- What footprint have I left in my life so far? How does it compare to others? How do I evaluate it? What do my rational considerations tell me? What does my gut feeling tell me?
- What are the potentials of my sustainability? What can I improve immediately and what later? What is my plan? How does the curve of my self-effective sustainability develop? How can I motivate myself emotionally in the process?
- How do I influence a change in the thinking of others not only rationally but also emotionally and practically? Which of my sustainable successes can best be turned into a narrative to inspire others?

Such individual narratives can also be even more powerful when paired with real nature experiences, bringing rewards for the new attitude, as it is then possible to see and feel what one is advocating. The more time we spend on nature experiences, on relationships, on art, on joint movement and health, the more we will spend on them in a versatile way and talk about them with others, thus opening up a new meaning of life. Part of the narrative could then be that we once again increasingly engage with things that cannot be bought, with events that give our world diversity instead of consuming simplicity. One aspect is particularly important here: Our narrative does not end in the arbitrary but in clear decisions for sustainable measures; we learn to align our behavior with goals for the common good.

Sustainability Needs Visions of the Future

How can we prevent even the sustainable from lying to themselves? Two prerequisites are necessary to actually achieve success in sustainability:

First, long-term planning and foresight, and courage to think far into the future and to make uncomfortable, firm, forward-looking decisions when problems first become perceptible rather than doing so only when events make them inevitable.

Second, a willingness to question core values and traditions of the previous society – such as fossil energies or superfluous consumption – as we have to say goodbye to such values and goals that were good and brought success in the past but are currently becoming counterproductive under changed conditions.

The Five Rs

If we want to self-effectively revolutionize sustainability on an individual level, then the five Rs are critical to counter our consumerism and negative footprint[23]:

1. *Refuse or reject:* Refraining from consumption, checking whether we really need something urgently (for example, wait 30 days between wanting to buy something and buying it when making a major purchase), rethinking our values and behaviors, and weighing what is important to us in life and what is superfluous.
2. *Reduce or downsize:* Less is more in sustainability. If we need something, how big, extensive, complete does it need to be? Part of having a sustainable mindset and self-efficacy is asking new questions: Is there a smaller, more sustainable solution? Can I share my consumption needs with others and thereby reduce my footprint?

3. *Reuse or repair:* Which products last longer? How do we go down the path of zero waste? How can we get companies to make goods that last? What can be fixed? Who can still use my discarded items? When do I buy secondhand? How do I exchange items that others can still use? In self-efficacy, it is crucial to feel joy and happiness when one's own sustainable contribution becomes visible, when it can be shown to others, when it inspires to go even more in this direction. We must relearn to feel a great joy not in new consumer goods, but above all in the recycling of what is already there and can be better and longer used.

4. *Recycle or reutilize:* The United States and European Union belong to the world champions of waste; everyone can change that. Recycling is one way, even if the infrastructure is not yet satisfactory enough. Nevertheless, I can arrange my life in such a way that I recycle as much as possible. Especially with textiles, this is against the trend but beneficial for the environment. This interferes with fashion and our self-reflections. When will it become chic and fashionable to openly display reutilization to the outside world? Wouldn't it be nice to demonstrate this openly within the sustainable community first?

5. *Rot or compost:* Throwing away food, living beyond one's means, sabotaging eco-cycles, this is a loss of control that still happens en masse today. Even those who do not have a garden can contribute to composting. There are no excuses. Fill the compost garbage can.

Create Your Own Infrastructure for the Development of Your Sustainable Actions!

The next dimension after building a sustainable attitude and steps into self-efficacy can unfold when an own infrastructure of sustainability is built and strengthened in the closer environment.

Strengthen Local Sustainability

People should be directly involved in the design of local infrastructures and have a say in what happens in their communities and the vicinity. We're a long way from that: As the owner of a property, I'm free to use renewable energy for heating and electricity. As a tenant, I can at least buy green electricity. There are far too few subsidies for such a conversion. I can also change my consumption to sustainability if there is an ecological and fair trade close to home, but this is associated with high costs. When I buy my food, I can support organic farming and fair labor conditions, avoid waste, keep water clean, and use it sparingly.

I can drive plastic and microplastics out of my life with significant effort, but even in helping to shape government provision for this, I am still subject to the dominance of a politics of unsustainability that has so far ensured that sustainable behavior remains the exception rather than the rule. After all, I have a vote in every election. I can use it.

In my individual actions, I, as a consumer at least, always have the chance to influence the supply and infrastructure through the demand for sustainable products and my own behavior. Individually, everyone can make a plan to make and expand their own infrastructure more sustainable (you will find a lot of updated help on the internet):

- How do I reduce the emissions I create in my household? How do I save energy? How do I avoid greenhouse gases?
- How do I limit and change my mobility so that I avoid fossil fuels and rely more on bicycles than cars? How do I make better use of public transport? How do I influence it toward sustainability in my community?
- How can I make my travel behavior more sustainable? What emissions will my next trip cause? What criteria do I use to decide whether I want to travel under such conditions?
- How do I reduce the consumption of raw materials? How do I find out which consumer goods consume how many raw materials, pollute the environment, or are produced under undignified working conditions, and what impact does this have on my bottom line? When I shop, do I consistently pay attention to Fairtrade? Do I choose textiles that can be used, exchanged, or reused for a long time? Do I use unpacked stores and do my children experience the fun of sorting unpacked goods themselves, storing them intelligently, and using them in a way that values them?
- How do I go about avoiding waste in my everyday life? What do I know about zero waste and possible strategies?[24] Do I avoid plastic wherever possible? Do I have my own reusable shopping bags? Where do I find microplastics in my household (such as in cosmetics) and what do I do about it? Do I fish microplastics out of my laundry?[25]
- How do I change my diet? How much do I gain by halving my meat consumption, how much by going vegetarian or vegan? Do I switch to organic products wherever possible to strengthen this area through my demand?
- What consumer goods do I really need? Does minimalism inspire me to look more closely at what I really need in life? How quickly do I want to replace old things with new ones? Which eco-burdens

become visible to me in the process? How do I deal with the fact that, as a rule, a higher income generates a significantly more negative footprint? What does my CO_2 calculator, which I find on the internet, tell me?

- How do I act politically so that a traffic turnaround finally takes place in my community, so that the state commits itself more clearly to sustainability, makes sustainable education mandatory in my children's schools, regulates the world in the direction of more sustainability?

No more excuses: We have to get politically involved locally and regionally in parties or nongovernmental organizations or other forms of organizations if we don't always want to leave the field to others! We have to organize our own sustainable infrastructure locally!

Being a Role Model for Sustainability

If we go this way, it is important that we pass on our convictions, that we carry the thoughts into the world to show that everyone can do something, that it is not hopeless, and that we are already many. How do the sustainable achieve the goal of all people turning to sustainability? Many people are already far in this third dimension of our sustainability agenda; we are already creating a sustainable infrastructure for ourselves. To do this, we had to take the first two steps: Get an overview, acquire sustainable knowledge, develop an attitude. And then have the first self-effective successes and recognize how it can be possible, even if only in the first small steps, to become more sustainable. In this way, the sustainable can already be a role model, show others ways, not simply dogmatically demand a change but personally encourage people to think about it and follow suit by telling them about successful experiences. The more they want to force others to do the same, the more they will have to reckon with refusals. The art of the sustainability narrative is to make others feel how urgent and important the task is. Unfortunately, the patience this requires in the face of approaching crises is not for the faint of heart.

Higher Costs Are Unavoidable

The majority of people in rich countries are still swimming along in the high tide of abundance, surrounded by an almost infinite number of consumer goods. A loss of this abundance would immediately convey the feeling of no longer being there, of no longer being able to keep up. The latest iPhone is only marginally different from its predecessor, but advertising suggests progress as technological miracles, an endless chain of wonders and desires constantly before our eyes. We generate endless waste through small differences, ever new objects of possession that swim with us in our high water of abundance, we flood the whole world with our consumption without yet possessing sufficient criteria for what is unavoidably necessary or simply superfluously chic.

Sustainability as renunciation is not sexy, it has no place in any action movie, but nevertheless, the number of many little hero stories increases, where minimalism and zero waste is practiced, a long flight is renounced, the consumption of meat is stopped, or the car is abandoned. It means a big challenge to finally overcome the ambivalence that arises the moment we agree with our own children when they attend Fridays for Future, only to order the vacation trip by cheap airplane or the new diesel in the next moment.

When we are faced with such ambivalences, we quickly think of others who are supposed to fix it: Isn't it the state's job to ensure sustainability? And why should I limit myself if no one else does?

We must not stop at this point but see clearly that we have a great influence on the course of events through our behavior. We can put pressure on capitalist society through our own consumer behavior and convince more people to do the same through our narratives. The more massively this happens, the greater the impact will be. All this will cost some; it will cause higher prices and a much higher effort, but the preservation of a livable environment should be worth it to us.

Align Your Consumption with Its Sustainability and Not with Low Prices!

When it comes to money, we enter a higher dimension of sustainability. As a basic principle, cheap prices unfortunately usually refer to the fact that the goods have been produced under unsustainable conditions. But what is sustainable consumption?

Sustainable consumption uses goods or services that satisfy needs without jeopardizing these opportunities for future generations. First and foremost, the environmental relevance of consumption must be taken into account; second, social aspects also play a role, insofar as they help to determine the future. Housing, food, and mobility are the three biggest factors that cause a negative ecological balance on an individual level today.[26] These three factors can be influenced by the market and consumer spending. The imperative is to make sustainability your status symbol. Prefer goods that are more durable than others, that have a better eco-balance; demand such goods on the markets; do not orientate yourself on seemingly cheap prices but think further: The cheap prices will cost us all dearly in the future. Again, knowledge is required because if you want more sustainability, you have to protect yourself from greenwashing,[27] which is often used to promise things that are not true at all. Another strategy is to simply keep quiet about the harmful effects.

Transforming Housing, Nutrition, and Mobility

Housing: When it comes to living, the residential building plays a key role. The building envelope can usually only be changed at great expense, but room heating and hot water, as well as electricity consumption, can also be controlled by behavior. Choose eco-providers and use household appliances and other electronic devices that seem ecologically sustainable, both in terms of the raw materials used and in terms of consumption; perhaps you can persuade the industry to make more sustainable offers here by giving preference to sustainable products.[28] Lighting can be made more energy-efficient. Overall, green power should become primary in every household, requiring the government and energy providers to enforce carbon-neutral technologies. Building renovation that addresses these changes without causing costs and rents to skyrocket is a major task for government funding, but also regulation is needed to become climate neutral.

Nutrition: In food, about one-third of the environmental impact comes from private households. Food production and supply contribute significantly to the increased formation of greenhouse gases.[29] Agriculture generates about half of total dietary greenhouse gas emissions, with animal foods accounting for a large share. Water consumption, pollution, species extinction, and soil erosion are major impacts of nonorganic agriculture in particular. Here, too, climate neutrality must be achieved through climate-neutral technologies, such as renewable energies, hydrogen, and bioenergies. And for consumer consumption, a switch to organic products is sustainable.

What can be done in detail? Reduce animal products and stimulants; don't buy greenhouse vegetables or air-freighted goods; prefer a vegetarian or vegan diet.[30] Above all, only buy what you can actually consume, so don't throw away food and always compost leftovers. A regional and seasonal diet also strengthens sustainability. Paying attention to your own body weight is not only good for your health but also for sustainability. A change in the amount of food eaten is enough to achieve significant sustainable effects: Less is always more!

Mobility: In the field of mobility, individual motorized traffic and truck transport is particularly harmful.[31] Here it helps to limit the use of cars as much as possible, to use public transport or car-sharing, to switch to an electric car (even if its eco-balance is not quite as positive as many people think),[32] and to avoid air travel and sea cruises as much as possible. The development of a comprehensive hydrogen technology is already a cost-effective way for ships, airplanes, and trucks, and in the future, it will also be able to achieve better effects for passenger cars than the purely electric car. Many jobs can now be done online from home. However, this increases electricity consumption, so it is urgently necessary to tie it to renewable energies.

Vote for Parties and Governments and Join Movements That See Sustainability as a Priority Task of the Present and Actually Want to Realize It!

In democratic decisions, majorities can err in what they do. They are often misled by the interests of a few. With respect to sustainability, scientifically reflective people today hope that majorities can be won that take risk analysis seriously and do not wait to act sustainably until they can no longer counter the negative effects of unsustainable action. But how can majorities be won over for something that depends primarily on changes in cherished habits, renunciation, and the dismantling of wishful thinking?

Climate Targets

In nature, there are in principle possibilities to constantly renew biomass, as shown by agricultural production, animal breeding, and fish reproduction, but the availability and purity of water, soil fertility owing to overfertilization, the consequences of factory farming, deforestation, compaction of land and soil, population growth, and other factors are currently influencing climate change negatively. On the other hand, there are technologies of regeneration and environmentally friendly production, which, however, have not yet been able to reverse the negative trend. Finding the individual indicators of change, evidence of progress or growing challenges, and modeling the process as it evolves is an arduous process, and we have to fight for much more support.[33]

Today, every person can calculate his or her own footprint quite accurately, and in many countries, there are corresponding tools on the internet. From the data, it can be seen that each individual in her or his household, through consumption and mobility, through diet and behavior, is always included in the chains of effects on greenhouse gases and thus climate change. According to Liverani,[34] individual households can be associated with about 35 percent of emissions in this regard, of which a good 30 percent could be saved very fast through energy-saving measures, which emphasizes the high responsibility of each individual in the crisis. While industry is clearly the main polluter in these cycles, it also directly or indirectly produces consumer goods for individual households.

Already the climate targets are difficult to implement because they contradict our capitalist way of life. To think, and even more to act, sustainably is the direct opposite of everything our actions are directed toward in everyday life: Prosperity, enjoyment, satisfaction, these are the terms that are associated with life and happiness today. Restriction, renunciation, paternalism, prohibitions, or levies for sustainable purposes, on the other hand, are associated with coercion, oppression, and injustice. But the path of avoiding action to save the planet imposes all burdens on the younger generation in their future. It is no wonder that younger people in particular are more critical of sustainability issues than their elders. Against the backdrop of such insight, the statement in politics that sustainability must be implemented in a socially compatible manner above all appears more as a survival strategy of the ruling political parties and the establishment. They do not dare to speak the truth: There can be no business as usual. The planet needs action that consistently gets to the roots of the wrong decisions. A fundamental rethinking of sustainability is inevitable!

Sustainable Must Win Majorities!

Every voice counts in sustainability; the sustainable are not yet in the majority, so they need to convince others to stand up for sustainability. There are already many, especially younger people, who think sustainably. But there are still too few, so joining a movement or starting your own is a task. It starts with the resistance against the apparent lack of alternatives of what is given! It is necessary to go beyond the individual dimensions, it is important to think and act in social groups in order to enforce sustainability more strongly in society as a whole. The will to truth is Janus-faced: If one side sees itself as the originator of human-made changes and their consequences for the future, the other side shrinks from this and looks for truths that can still give humanity a lot of time to save the old habits and quite a few hope for fast scientific-technological progress. Since humanity comes from an age of lacking sustainability, it seems to be overwhelmed to face the new problem and is still looking for solutions from the successful past.

Question All News!

The information about the world and the news are all wildly juxta-posed today, and it is tedious to sort them out and question them. Everyone should, that is the democratic claim, choose for themselves from this conglomerate, which has always been shaped by interest groups and the consumer society. In this collection of information and reports, it is difficult to find one's own overview to distinguish facts from distortions. There is no indisputable set of facts about sustain-ability because pluralism is always about interpretations, discussions, opinions, and counter-opinions, all presented side by side. For sustain-ability, it is important to learn to distinguish between facticity – what we hold to be factual and true – and validity – what majorities and institutions or governments hold to be true and valid in their rules and laws, regulations, and established rules. Validity determines what indi-vidual nations determine to be the "truth" of their program based on their interpretation of the facts about, say, the climate crisis. Although the individual can critically question which motives are behind state or political action in order to critically confront the powers of opin-ion, he or she is at the same time confronted with a mainstream that includes interpretive sovereignties. Only in a critical stance does it then become apparent that all information is always already subject to cer-tain interpretations with selective interests.

This becomes very clear, for example, in the case of definitions of limit values. Limits indicate the values above which something is harm-ful, so they can actually be measured quite clearly by the sciences. But what if the limit values are embellished, manipulated by the influence of lobbyists, and unambitious politics? What if the set values are signifi-cantly detrimental to health because politicians want, for example, to protect the car industry? What if it is primarily about economic interests and not health interests? The diesel scandal with the fraud of the car manufacturers shows how safe customers are supposed to feel when they only look at the claimed values but are unable to see the fraud behind them. And in which sales field can we still be sure today not to be cheated? Why does the state, if it is supposed to serve the general public and common good, not adequately protect us from such fraud?

Make Sustainable Alliances!

It is undeniable, individually and in a manageable living environ-ment, everyone can already do a lot for sustainability, they can do it for themselves, their children, friends, they can do it on a local level in immediate relationships with a lot of commitment. But at the same time, they know that sustainability concerns a global world and therefore needs further means and ends. Just as they have initially informed themselves about their negative footprint, built up their own attitude and self-efficacy, organized and designed an infrastructure in their environment, and oriented themselves less on prices and more on sustainable effects, they have to take a further step and look at who else stands for sustainability besides themselves and their direct relationships. Now the question arises, How can their own convictions be translated into a larger political dimension? What alliances can be forged?

There are many questions about the right way: Is it enough to go to the polls to give a voice to those who promise more sustainability? It is a first step. A second would be to get involved in a political party. Here, however, one is subject to dominant currents of political opinion within the respective party. Is extra-parliamentary opposition a good way to achieve greater sustainability? It is always necessary, at least, because parties often freeze once they are in power and want to maintain it. Are nongovernmental organizations the best way to fight for sustainability with clear actions? They are necessary to get powerfully into concrete and spontaneous action. All these ways are useful to do something for sustainability – there is not one right way; rather, you have to find your own ways: No matter how one chooses, it is essential for strengthening sustainability that one does not remain alone and thereby run the risk of thinking that nothing can be achieved anyway. In the struggle for sustainability, the sustainable must stand together against all those who want to continue to destroy the planet relentlessly. The nonsustainable must be convinced either by arguments or by exemplary deeds. If that is not enough, then the only option is to outvote them.

Fight for an Enlightened and Sustainable Education, Politics, Science!

The first five dimensions have emphasized individual responsibility, focusing on what each and everyone can do to fight for sustainability. For these individual factors, the social is always implicitly significant, but now concrete social ideas have to be explicitly developed, it has to be asked how society as a whole can be transformed into a sustainable one.

In order to strengthen sustainability, it is first of all an urgent task to get the state, the media, and the public to provide all people with comprehensive education and enlightenment about sustainability on a scientific basis![35] Learning for sustainability must become a priority in all educational institutions and in the media because this is the central task of humanity in this century! This includes a comprehensive education about the global boundaries of Earth, about the dangers of all aspects of missing sustainability. At the same time, recommendations for sustainable behavior have to be anchored in the practices and routines of social life, communicated in institutions, and tested practically! There must be manifold programs of sustainable education for all groups of people; for a change of sustainable behavior, there must be an advertisement for sustainability, which at the same time socially rewards successes in sustainability with recognitions and opportunities for advancement.

Scientifically Understand the Starting Position

So what can we hope for? The sciences must come more to the fore. There is the natural science view, such as on the states of climate, water, and resources. From this perspective, like that given by the Intergovernmental Panel on Climate Change, we learn the facts of the crisis. Another approach is formed by social, economic, and political studies, which discuss the relationship of sustainability to the human economy and way of life in a variety of ways.[36] Philosophical, cultural, and ethical considerations provide an interpretive framework for assessing sustainability issues. But sustainability is not a continuous idea in these traditions and must always be emphasized first. Political-economic discourses combine ecological criticism with a critique of capitalism.[37] The public discourse in the media and governmental statements is determined in particular by the UN and its sub-organizations, as well as some leading nongovernmental organizations. This has given rise to a field of political ecology in which diverse interest groups gather.[38]

Overall, the multiplicity of approaches in scientific publications and professional societies – particularly in the natural sciences – accelerates scientific assessment, which can contribute to objectification by determining demonstrable changes and tipping points that help us to understand the situation. Whether such understanding can lead to changing people's behavior, is, however, a completely different question. There are serious doubts about this because the already existing scientific data have so far failed to have a sufficient effect on the majority of humanity, especially on politics. This raises the question of whether this can be achieved at all through arguments or whether major catastrophes with experienced tipping points have to set in before the majority of people can be persuaded to consider the limits to growth and to act sustainably.

But when these tipping points actually occur, it will be too late for an effective change of course because the time window for really effective countermeasures is then closed. Major compromises will then be made. What complicates the situation is the fact that it has proven difficult to give precise time lines with accurate forecasts in complex issues with very many variables whose solutions can only ever lie in statements about probabilities. Climate deniers in particular draw a profit from this but also supporters of progress conjecture that there are enough "truths" for a present that may not be perfect but is safe and worth living in, and that can be saved by progress and viable solutions alone.[39] From this, people like to conclude that everything is better than we have assumed so far[40] or that Western reason with its idea of enlightenment gives us hope that we can always make it.[41]

The Lack of Education about Sustainability Must End!

Basically, many people today already sense what would have to be done to improve sustainability in education. Sustainability at least has meanwhile arrived in the media, still as one topic among many others, but it is not yet mandatory in all school curricula. Neither is the complexity of the topic in learning compulsory for all learners, nor are decision-makers from politics, business, science, and relevant interest groups prepared to enforce the topic comprehensively enough in the education system. Many people remain largely uneducated in the long term. In particular, sacrifices are taboo, and pipe dreams of perpetual growth without demonstrable regenerative technologies that could lead to reversal effects are fantasized in order to reassure the public. Many are already shying away from Fridays for Future. Yet they are the ones who are boldly and honestly addressing reality: We must phase out fossil fuels immediately and meet climate targets according to scientific standards, or our planet is beyond saving! These learners are far ahead of the teachers!

Overcoming Obstacles to Sustainable Education!

The knowledge of the world is divided into school subjects, which in turn are not weighted according to important and less important topics. Especially three constructions in education condition a structure that hinders a necessary sustainable awareness:[42]

1. *More and more new content and no prioritization:* The sciences always generate new content through new research results, which lead them into specializations. But what of this knowledge is necessary for all? How are sustainable decisions to be made convincingly if there are already no clear prioritizations in education

but specialized topics that stand additively next to each other? Specialized knowledge is particularly necessary in concrete applications in the social division of labor – for example, in certain professions or for certain problems. But what of it do all adolescents need in general education, and what material should they be able to choose according to their interests and inclinations? Which subjects should be compulsory for all, and where should they be allowed to opt-out or go into greater depth? In a school focused on knowledge, the question of selecting relevant material for future life and thus addressing the pressing changes of the time has been lost through the overabundance of content. The old subject divisions of school subjects can no longer reflect the requirements of today's world in their diversity and change. There is already a blind trust that even highly specialized school subject knowledge will meet a need at some time and somewhere, but countries that prefer knowledge reproduction refuse to deselect school subjects, as well as to deepen electives according to the challenges of real living conditions. To give more importance to relevant topics for life and thus also to sustainability, all countries need a sustainable education and prioritization of sustainable topics. This means establishing interdisciplinary issues that replace or supplement previously rigid school subjects. The use of applied, experimental, and investigative methods is necessary to help build an appropriate understanding of science that can critically distinguish scientific results from fake news. Let's follow after more than 100 years the Deweyan way of education.[43] Increased engagement with probabilities, risk analysis, and behavioral barriers is important, including reflection on one's own behavior, and, overall, stronger participation of all learners in the selection of what they should learn.

2. *A too-narrow understanding of methods and competencies:* In many countries, frontal teaching still dominates methodologically. Knowledge is imparted in a rather schematic way. The subject contents are all in sequence and juxtaposed, but the inner context, a holistic understanding, and problem-solving are limited to a small knowledge transfer, which promotes too few competencies of researching, independent, and creative learning. Critical to this system is that too much is taught in text forms. Quantity too often takes precedence over quality. Thus one thinks to have a good concept of general education, although in practice it is then only a matter of piecemeal knowledge, which is too little to form a competence and application understanding of the problems of one own's life and the global world. Education should

help to solve problems instead of merely memorizing the problem solutions of teachers or textbooks. There are deficits, especially in research-based learning. The opportunities for exemplary, holistic, and experimental learning with cross-thematic questions and problems remain too much unused. However, this is indispensable for an understanding of sustainability issues.

3. *Too little application:* Furthermore, the addition of a lot of material and the methodical narrowing of knowledge transfer in the education system leads to a dramatic increase in the superficiality of learning and a considerable decrease in experimental or application-related approaches. Scientific work is not learned by reproducing scientific results in knowledge quizzes but only through exemplary scientific work of one's own, which can make the scientific methods understandable and verifiable in experience and with experienced results. A radical reform here is necessary to connect important basic questions of natural sciences, technology, medicine, health, and sustainability with questions of economics, politics, and other disciplines. This is to provide diverse and broad access to scientific work. This should also include the larger social issues that relate to the challenges of sustainability. A superficial level of understanding is overcome only when case-based and concrete problems are explored and reasoned results are achieved. A sufficient awareness to distinguish facts from fake news will only emerge if fact-checking is always built into all learning content as far as possible. This, above all, can later protect learners from populist simplifications and conspiracy theories.

We Need a Radically New Concept of Learning for Sustainability!

A scientific commission of experts beyond all school bureaucracies and individual scientific interests, beyond party politics, but with the participation of learners and parents, should develop a list of topics that stands for a new general education, whereby common basic competencies (compulsory topics) are distinguished from competencies according to interests and inclinations (optional topics). Again, we can still learn from Dewey because he foresaw for democratic education what is needed in crises like the present one: It is prioritizing the involvement of learners in all aspects of their learning and to give them chances to participate. In addition, according to international research, the goal should be a community school for all in order to take advantage of the opportunities offered by heterogeneous learning groups over the longest possible periods of time, as Scandinavia in particular is doing successfully.[44] The school system must be consistently inclusive in order to give all adolescents better educational opportunities.

Furthermore, it should be made clear to the public that today's education cannot represent the breadth of existing knowledge; it must concentrate on imparting especially basic knowledge and an understanding of scientific work for fundamental problems and existential questions. Results of psychological behavioral research on sustainability should always be included in educational concepts and implementations.[45] Teachers would need to be more competently prepared for their learners than they are now in order to teach well. So far, the dominance of the disciplines in terms of content has often put the content before all preoccupations with questions of educational psychology, learning research, communication, and comprehensive methodological training. The question applies to all countries: In an age of lifelong learning, how can teachers not be comprehensively trained in pedagogy and psychology? How can it be, in an age of rapid change and great challenges, that the curricula in many places are predominantly overfilled with material from the past or specialized knowledge and omit the essential questions of the present? How can it be that questions of human health, the economy, social problems, democratic risks, fake news, the manipulation of knowledge and opinions, but above all sustainability, are not at the center of school?

We Need a Radically New Media Concept!

Even if it is an exaggeration to speak of a constant press of lies or of the media being brought into line, the fact is that the media are influenced in many ways and in some cases do not take a very close look at the scientifically based truth. Even the public broadcasters – if they still exist – are under the influence of political parties and have an inner scissor in their heads that regulates what seems permissible, desirable, and appropriate. In the case of private media operators, this influence is directly controlled by the selective interests of the owners. Against this background, information is prepared by the media as a mixture, often characterized by pseudo-experts, one-sided presentation, or dramatization of details. This leads to the omission of essential connections, the emphasis on extremes in sensationalism, and a dualistic way of thinking that is supposed to create clarity but often only means thinking in black and white. Media depend on increasing circulation, which repeatedly leads them into overemphasis on deviations, outrage journalism, and even conspiracies. Moreover, information tends to be arbitrarily juxtaposed, which is considered democratic as a pluralistic dissemination of opinion. But what becomes relevant news in such a system? During the coronavirus pandemic, for example, most other issues took a back seat. Why was sustainability, as an existential issue of the present, not given the same prominence? The sustainable media offensive we need means a turnaround in the media itself. A return to investigative, honest, and background-revealing journalism, which has become too rare. The public broadcasters, too, have a duty to offer this to the public more democratically than before, beyond their party-political supervisory interests and beyond partisanship. Science-based journalism that clearly states truths and necessities and does not constantly relativize them can lead to a change in opinion formation toward a more science-based approach.

We Need Free and Independent Research!

But how free are the sciences to produce neutral and objective results beyond mere desires or selective interests? Scientifically based results cannot simply be derived from objects or nature itself, as common sense likes to assume. The rainforest is factually present, but at the same time, the sciences add to it, for example, by using standardized procedures of description, observation, analysis, and modeling. These research procedures can therefore produce solid and comprehensible results, insofar as they are repeatable and allow objective statements to be made in agreement between different research disciplines and groups. This alone is difficult enough. But if these researches are financed by donors with certain expectations on the results, because results are desired for the benefit of certain interests, then the research has to fear for the correctness of the research results.[46] Scientific success, which today is increasingly measured by how much money can be raised privately for research, even at public universities, faces constant temptation to forget its own claim to truth.

Against this background, it becomes clear that a fundamental shift to sustainable imagining and thinking as a prerequisite for sustainable action will only succeed if researchers can be concerned with the research itself. A hoped-for benefit to prosperity or economic profits must not determine research. If we analyze, for example, the current practice of the UN's sustainability efforts, we can see an attitude that wants to continue the existing prosperity in order to slow down climate change and resource depletion with it and not against it. This one-sided starting position, based on wishes and expectations of growth, is also readily propagated by the media, but it is also misleading. For ever-increasing growth is always the problem to solve and makes the solution more difficult or even impossible. Scientific research shows where more sustainability would have to take place immediately because the damage is greater than assumed. This will not please many in business and politics or any science they finance. But we need honest answers!

Neutral research that is as objective as possible, committed to sustainability, and not geared to one-sided economic interests or national egoisms is becoming increasingly necessary in order to identify hitherto neglected sustainable problems and to develop truthful solutions. At the same time, it is also necessary to translate the results of scientific research into comprehensible everyday language. Funding programs for this purpose are necessary, just as the protection of research from interference by business and politics is indispensable. Priority must be given to research that not only generates profits but can also strengthen sustainability and human health.[47] The orientation of scientific careers and rewards beyond profit interests and individual enrichment requires a comprehensively financed public science system that grants independence through income and freedom of research. De jure this is enshrined in higher education law in many places, but de facto this is constantly being circumvented where economic interests come into play. The way has been paved for these developments wherever the state does not provide sufficiently comprehensive funding for a free system of science and has driven it into the hands of private third-party funding.

Increase the Value of Science

Moreover, such an independent science would also have to be instrumental in translating the findings into laws and regulations; the findings must not be reinterpreted either in individual countries or by particularistic politics in order to achieve national or selective advantages in preserving the old ways. The question is whether humanity can and will submit to such reason, or whether the old and proven competition for advantages against others will remain dominant. The scientific path can succeed honestly and objectively only if science is given a higher value in all places, if it is valued as an independent force, and if humanity moves into a scientific age and thus opposes the superficial material culture of consumption with a strategy in which the curiosity for knowledge is put before the profanity of ever-more profits or consumer needs that harm the limits of the earth.

Taking Sides for Sustainability!

If we take all these demands together, then environmental parties with a clear ecological profile correspond to them most closely. Unfortunately, however, these party programs do not mean that the demands formulated there will be implemented: Often, the promised prioritization of ecology is quickly forgotten once the parties gain power. Thus, a policy of empty words quickly emerges as soon as it is a matter of gaining or maintaining one's own established power. At present, many parties outdo each other in their ecological promises, only to then simultaneously berate the Greens for supposedly wanting too much. Quite a few sustainable people are frustrated by empty promises and therefore seek extra-parliamentary groups. Working and having an impact outside of parties is an important corrective to exerting critical pressure on parties. But it is also clear that sustainability is determined, managed, and steered toward global politics via parliaments at the national level first. Therefore, for the fight for more sustainability, the sustainable must not shy away from the walk through the institutions, as arduous as it is because here the decisions are made for all!

Fight for Laws, Regulations, and Controls in the Sense of Sustainability!

An essential and still underdeveloped dimension is that the state must actively and preventively ensure sustainability through environmental and health laws, regulations, and controls instead of shifting responsibility to individual sustainable actions alone or simply letting the economy do its thing. The climate does not follow stock prices, resource depletion does not decrease when people make their lifestyles more luxurious, biodiversity does not increase when the world becomes easier to travel. Human desires are in sharp contrast to the environment they conquer, the climate they alter, the resources they consume, the species they destroy. Today, we have reached a point where it is clear that our desires depend on the environment we destroy. If there is no fertile soil to live on, no air to breathe, no water to drink, all other desires become impossible. We must rethink our behavior. If our children wantonly destroy our home, we would admonish them and try to educate them, but if the children ask us why we wantonly destroy their world, we simply shrug our shoulders. We must finally wake up and act: Rethink education, economy, ecology completely, and dare a new beginning!

We Need a Sustainability Treaty!

So far, humanity, out of its liberal history of the last centuries and the struggle of the economic lobbyists, lacks the assertive instruments to make regulations and controls binding on the basis of laws and enforceable rights. With respect to the environment, health, and sustainability, there is a national lack of a fundamental right that could give rise to further regulations. But fundamental rights are tricky because everyone would already have a right to equality today, but this is undermined from the outset by the inequality of initial conditions. Laws and regulations would have to define very precisely what health and a protected environment mean in each individual case, limit values would have to be determined, permitted deviations would have to be defined, penalties for violations would have to be established. And all of this would then have to be expanded from a national agenda to a global agreement. A utopia? Not at all because this idea is not impossible but just not yet implemented. It is easy to see from the rapid and goal-oriented implementation of the coronavirus measures, as well as the money raised, what is possible – even if it is not perfect but already the possibility was dismissed as impossible beforehand. That is why it is important to win new political majorities to demand the sustainability contract. However, coronavirus has also shown that national solutions still dominate. The biggest challenge in the future will be that all people all over the world think about the common good globally and no longer just nationally!

We Need Regulations, Controls, and Penalties!

What is needed today, above all, are environmental laws and the regulations associated with them, higher consumption and emission standards, ecological building standards, energy-saving regulations, regulations for the protection of health, regulations in the production of goods in the case of raw materials, in the case of energy savings and ecological compatibility, in the case of environmental toxins, in the distribution of all raw materials and goods in harmony with the environment, in the disposal, and in the quality control of all consumer goods. Regulations are needed in all these areas because higher prices and taxes alone will not be enough to turn things around quickly and broadly enough. In the case of the particularly harmful effects on sustainability, it is a matter of intensively and continuously checking that rules of sustainability are observed in accordance with the state of scientific impact research to identify harm. Such regulation includes the establishment of independent scientific institutions that establish a canon of rules of negative sustainable effects that must be avoided at all costs and set standards on what must be banned or given limits. At the same time, there must be effective controls and very high penalties for violations of bans and limits for polluters!

When we talk about sustainable development in the sense of the UN Global Goals, we have to ask what exactly is to be developed. Is it the limits of growth that are to be respected or the progress of growth that is to help ensure that the changes are not quite as damaging as they will be in the future? How damaging may the effects be, how great the overstepping of the boundaries? To what new battleground zones will the damage be shifted so that prosperity grows and new profitable technologies emerge?

The global goals of the UN may all be desirable in themselves, but in the internal context, they raise very critical questions. They always sidestep the ecological question where the social solution is prioritized, but its ecological consequences are not further addressed. What would it mean ecologically if we abolished poverty as quickly as possible? What consumption, what damage by masses of people would result if the formerly poor also wanted to live like those who have caused the great ecological damage until today? If these questions are asked by those who already live in rich countries, they must seem cynical. After all, who can deny participation to those whose consumer freedoms are only now beginning – who finally also want to buy, travel, and live in abundance? From the point of view of the earth's boundaries, this would have to be offset by a renunciation in all countries. But who will be willing to do this for reasons of fairness? Many of the UN goals focus on the development progress that is economically hopeful and socially desirable but ecologically not thought through in the interactions. The desired transformation is more complex than can be represented in global goals without system thinking. Chabay identifies three reasons that make sustainable development goals (SDGs) difficult:[48]

First, the SDGs represent a set of critical issues and problems that are highly interconnected and interdependent. They can mainly be presented in individual segments for illustrative purposes, but in practice, they should be addressed holistically and with systemic models because the goals are far-reaching, interact with each other, and there are no easy solutions.[49]

Second, the goals always assume that the socioeconomic reality of contemporary capitalism is the only basis for a solution without sufficiently discussing at which points this becomes self-contradictory and where and how this could be counteracted. Here the compromise character of the UN strategy and the enforcement character of economically strong countries becomes apparent.

Third, the political structure of the signatory countries of the goals is left out. But between these political governments – between democracies and authoritarian regimes – there are inevitably contradictions between national and global goals, allegiances in ownership, democratic and despotic ways of living, expectations of prosperity, and commitments to the planet and its boundaries. The question of how sustainable policies can succeed appears as a fundamental question that will be experienced in the implementation of the SDGs as a tension between ambitious goals and desirable narratives in the national context and actual deeds and their effects for renunciation and change.

Against this background, it seems useful to fight for sustainability to express two perspectives: On the one hand, all people are concerned as learning beings in all age groups, so it is the task of lifelong sustainable learning and education to ensure the path toward sustainability.[50] On the other hand, the idea of development, which is always associated with capitalist growth, must be freed from the asumed attachment to sustainability, because we must approach the problem more openly.[51]

What to Do Immediately for Climate Neutrality!

Scientific analyses show a clear path for climate neutrality. If one follows the recommendations that are available today in the climate debate, then some benchmarks are unavoidably to be met; they essentially correspond to the demands of Fridays for Future, Extinction Rebellion, or Greenpeace:

For climate-neutral rich countries, emissions would have to fall at least 65 percent below 1990 levels by 2030. One hundred percent would be better! This means a major shift to renewable energy, huge investments in technologies like hydrogen, and electrification (but only with green electricity) of buildings and transportation to force the abandonment of fossil fuels. The fossil age has to end as quickly as possible!

Building on this, climate-neutral technologies would need to be deployed to achieve at least another 95 percent in reductions as soon as possible but no later than 2045. The remaining emissions must be offset by capturing and storing CO_2 with climate technology measures.

However, the national path alone will not be enough, although rich countries can play a pioneering role here – certainly with technological and economic advantages. Internationally, many measures need to be taken in the same direction. Imports and exports, supply chains, and trade agreements must be linked to sustainability obligations in order to enforce them worldwide. However, targets alone will not help to become climate neutral. Measures must be taken to ensure that clear pricing and regulations bring the achievement of targets to the forefront and impose penalties for noncompliance on all responsible parties in business and politics.

It must also be remembered, however, that sustainability is more than climate. In all areas of sustainability, such as resource depletion, species extinction, water pollution, and poisoning of the world, and other problems, regulations and interventions are necessary that prioritize scientific insights and place them above the wishful thinking and power of certain elites and interest groups. In addition, the production of weapons of mass destruction must be countered through peace efforts and international treaties rather than allowing their numbers to continue to grow.

We Must Limit Lobbyism!

The capitalist system has no interest in sustainability; on the contrary: Whole crowds of lawyers, lobbyists, and publicists argue tirelessly for an "always-on" approach. In the debates, more and more good-sounding goals are proclaimed, but the arguments on the side of those who then favor pro-business solutions or obtain exceptions weigh heavier and heavier in the end. This is not because they are actually more convincing but because their advocates have more influence, more power, and more money. In this way, a necessary change is permanently prevented!

A lobbying register – nationally and globally – should and could prevent this. But would that be enough? Is it not rather time that the democratically elected institutions commit themselves to the higher value of the common good in all issues and above all in sustainability? Shouldn't there be an overall agreement on this that, despite all the differences in party interests, at least guarantees that one-sided interests are not directly enforced against health, against an ecology of survival? And shouldn't citizens be able to sue for this if it is violated?

A new catalog of laws, which regulates sustainability concretely first for individual countries and then later globally for all, could finally put an end to the empty promises! If, for example, it becomes apparent in the supply chain that workers are working in an inhumane manner and that the environment is being poisoned, then not only the people in the distant countries would have to be given the right to sue but also consumers would have to be able to sue the companies that import such goods. It would force nations and, in the long run, the world community – through internationally binding laws – to finally act responsibly on all sides. Legislative powers would then also have to agree on which means of control and punishment to choose. In individual nations, majorities are enough to do this. But to achieve this globally, unanimity is needed in the UN, which would then also have to be given an executive mandate to enforce the measures against all. As long as that doesn't exist, we are lying to ourselves. We hope that if we keep waiting or make small progress within individual nations, the problems will go away. We lie to ourselves when we decide more and more without actually implementing it. The lie is that we want to just get on with the day-to-day, to continue to suppress the magnitude of the challenge, to not use institutional authority that allows for clear commitments. We reassure ourselves when we see an increase in wind turbines and solar panels nationally, instead of dealing with greenhouse gases that continue to rise globally. This constant sugarcoating and reassurance must stop, honest action is needed now!

A basic human right to survive in a sustainable environment could be a start. Reconstruct human rights! From this, many other rights can be derived, which must be declared binding, so that we can concretely claim our chances of survival – at least in democratic countries. And against this background, the democratic countries must become much more involved in the global struggle for sustainability, especially in trade and economic relations!

Fight for a Public Infrastructure That Comprehensively Strengthens Sustainability for All!

A socio-ecological transformation, which is intended by sustainable development, is so challenging because already the respective starting conditions are different.[52] Humans, in historically evolved social structures, are highly dependent on the natural and cultural world in which they live. Their relationship to the respective environment determines attitudes, perspectives, and expectations via the social development process; it drives what is considered valuable, relevant, and indispensable in a society and culture. Already from this starting position, people react very differently to the necessary transformation process in the face of planetary boundaries.

Water, energy, and transportation are sources and carriers of economic development because they are used extensively in production and distribution, services, and leisure.

Save the Clean Water!

Water: Clean tap water is as essential as food for all of us. In the USA, water consumption per capita is 400 liters, even Germany with 122 liters still has a very high consumption. It is a weakness of the water supply that drinking water and industrial water are not differentiated.

Thus drinking water becomes wastewater; for many water uses, drinking water is wasted, where rain and industrial water would be completely sufficient. In the household and even more in trade and industry, water is polluted, especially by pollutants and microplastics. This must be countered by individual reductions in their own water consumption, while at the same time trade and industry must be regulated even more strongly in the direction of sustainability. Water protection is poor in many countries; in particular, small bodies of water are often excluded from mandatory compliance with environmental targets; in many countries, environmental targets are not justified and measures to achieve them are inadequately planned. As a result, water quality deteriorates. It is important for all countries to establish a sustainable infrastructure with national regulations and to implement traceable measures to improve the water status. The protection of coastal waters and seas is an urgent task across national borders. We finally need a uniform approach to water protection!

Consistently Implement the Energy Turnaround!

Energy: The realization of the energy turnaround has long stagnated in many rich countries. In surveys, people from different countries say it is too expensive and implementation is chaotic; it is unfair in pricing because everyone has to pay for the industry; it would only have a positive impact on a minority.[53] The conversion to wind energy could be faster, bureaucratic hurdles and lack of government provision for power lines are well known; they have an effect especially in countries where politicians have not yet made a priority commitment to sustainability. Surveys show that many people in the richer countries would accept higher electricity costs if the levy were also fairer. In addition, many would prefer photovoltaics, but this change has so far been held back politically by insufficient subsidy policies. It has a particularly negative effect if CO_2 prices levied today flow into the budgets of the countries and not specifically into projects for a sustainable infrastructure. If CO_2 prices are levied, then they must not be used economically, for example, for climate-damaging investments; they would have to be invested in sustainability in a strictly demonstrable manner. The USA, China, and other rich countries are characterized by a shockingly poor ecological record.

We Need the Traffic Turnaround Now!

Transport: With regard to transport and travel, sustainable mobility would have to be supported, while environmentally harmful ones would have to be made more expensive. All political parties basically know today that especially individual traffic can be slowed down by more and cheaper public transport. Emission-based traffic control with speed limits and driving bans, and closing inner cities to cars could have a high impact on reducing greenhouse gases. But parties often keep quiet about environmental truths. Overall, there is also a need for cost-intensive strengthening of energy-efficient technologies, construction of passive houses, renovation of the old stock, and other measures that help strengthen sustainability. In the age of digitalization, unnecessary travel should also be reduced through increased work in the home office and simplifications in administration promoted through digitalization. At the same time, it is important to compensate for increased electricity consumption through greater expansion of renewable energies. Continuous renewable energy generation is necessary in the infrastructure to satiate the hunger for energy that exists still and will increase dramatically in the age of sustainability. In legislation, the common good must be emphasized much more strongly over private interests so that the infrastructure can be expanded broadly enough and without constant objections.

Such infrastructure is the responsibility of all countries. A change in policy can be achieved in elections alone. All sustainable people are called upon to recognize in the party programs where empty promises are to be found, how so far infrastructure has been poorly developed or neglected by whom, who is responsible for the poor balance sheets, and how it can be achieved that things will be better in the future. We all experience how the climate changes, how heat and heavy rain increase, how a lack of raw materials becomes visible, and how many species disappear. But are we also aware of which parties and people are responsible for this? Do we seriously want to keep electing them as our political representatives?

Fight for Pricing of All Nonsustainable Consumer Goods and Services!

In addition to necessary regulation through rules and laws, a pricing of the lack of sustainability is necessary. In a capitalist society, price has a decisive influence on purchasing behavior. In this sense, the price of harmful things should become higher to the extent that human behavior harms the environment, the climate, the world's resources, and all other sustainability factors. There should also be government bans on products with particularly harmful effects.

Prices are the same for everyone, and so seem fair. But they are not, because the ability to pay them depends on money, which is socially very unequally distributed. Take air travel, which is particularly harmful to the climate under current conditions. A sensible, sustainable policy would have to tax air travel very heavily, thereby curbing it. At the same time, more environmentally friendly alternatives would have to be promoted and given low prices.[54] But such a measure would be deeply unfair to many people. Those who have already traveled the world can sit back and say, well, I've seen it all. But those who have yet to travel, who have yet to discover the world in all its diversity, would be banned and denied expensive air travel. This will seem unfair to them. And at the same time, high fares will again overreach the rich, who, for example, can already afford first-class travel, which is unaffordable for others.

However, people will, unfortunately, have to live with such injustices in sustainability, because there is simply no alternative today if we still want to save our planet. A fair distribution system in the increase of costs and shortage of opportunities, a system of subsidies and compensation could become the program of political parties in the future, which want to look for a social balance here. Further down, the solution offered is to use a fair tax system in conjunction with the higher prices. Nevertheless, the amount of harmful actions will have to be strictly limited.

It is clear that low-income people will not be able to shoulder the sustainability costs alone in the existing system. But it is equally clear that the distribution of existing wealth has been completely unjust for some time, so there is plenty of scope for redistribution. Higher wages and better incomes for the previously socially disadvantaged are necessary to pay the higher prices. To achieve sustainability fairly for all, a reform of the entire distribution system will be needed and the rich and super-rich will have to participate more!

Determination of Ecologically Harmful Baskets of Goods

How should sustainable prices be formed? Before sustainability can be priced, independent scientific determinations are needed as to how much missing sustainability there is in individual baskets of goods. The consumer goods in question would have to be comprehensively classified and certified as to their sustainability. Although producers will say that this is impossible, unfair, and not even calculable, in sustainability, it is not an economic but an ecological principle that applies: Every product, regardless of its production costs and sales prices, has an ecological balance that can be determined with scientific objectivity. A certified baseline for pricing can be achieved. Analogous to how the energy consumption of an appliance is visible in a table, all consumer goods could carry a label of their sustainability.

Three sets of measures are unavoidable if the lack of sustainability is to be defeated:

First, a census of all products that are particularly harmful to greenhouse gases and other aspects of the lack of sustainability. The recording and determination must be independent of economic and national money benefits and subsequently serve to certify ecological products and label environmental quality, such as eco-labels and sustainability balances of the products and services concerned, so that they can then be given premiums or discounts in pricing. In addition to the value-added tax, an environmental tax could increase prices for individual classes of damage. The current emissions trading system is an inadequate instrument because it distributes the burdens in the world too little according to verified ecological aspects, and it allows for the possibility that richer people buy their way out of damages they cause. As a result of the individual provisions, the revenue generated by surcharges could then be returned to environmental and nature conservation – for example, in reforestation via the state in a legally regulated manner. The increased price is also an opportunity for consumers to offset the negative effects of their consumption by using part of the price.

Second, a price on the pollution and environmental contamination of the world. The higher the pollution limits are exceeded, the higher the prices. If the limits are exceeded more, then this should be punished with high fines and even imprisonment. Prices must also be set for urban sprawl and sealing, violations of species, water protection, and resource consumption for nonrenewable raw materials. The lack of sustainability is often not immediately visible in individual products, but it can be determined in terms of its impact and, here too, surcharges can be applied according to damage classes. At the same time, sustainable alternatives would have to be made cheaper and promoted in order to stimulate alternative production and lifestyles.

Third, decent work or pay in the producing countries could also be achieved through surcharges and fair production certification. This would force all countries to initiate their own improvements. A right to sue for sustainability and fair trade in the affluent countries against the companies that earn money from such products would be more effective than waiting for something to change in the places of origin with poor production. In order to work globally in the sense of human dignity and sustainable ecological production, we must fight for nationally enforceable rights, which we can enforce against a neoliberal economic and lobby policy.

Social Security for the Poorer People

The necessary pricing of nonsustainable goods would currently impose a burden on low-income earners that would be almost impossible to bear. But this does not mean at all that it is not possible – it is absolutely unavoidable! Rather, it means that these people must receive an income that can absorb the higher costs of sustainability. In pricing, the struggle for more sustainability becomes a struggle for social security for the majority of lower-wage groups and incomes. There are numerous ideas in the sustainability discussion on how this could be achieved.[55] First, wages or basic income in social security would have to be adjusted to the cost of the current sustainable basket of goods. In any case, the social imbalance in incomes has yet to be evened out because socially a low-wage sector has spread, driving many people into precarious and undignified working and living conditions. If a sustainable turnaround is sought through pricing, then a socioeconomic reform of wages and incomes is inevitable, especially in the case of precarious conditions. The sustainability crisis holds up a mirror of its economic imbalance to society!

Fight for a Legal and Tax System That Rewards Sustainability!

If sustainability is to succeed, then a radical reversal is needed, a legal and tax system that clearly prioritizes sustainability. If humanity is to survive, it must do so first nationally as a model for others but as quickly as possible internationally and globally. There have been many ideas in the history of capitalism on how taxation could be implemented to achieve more social justice. Radical was the idea in the "Communist Manifesto," to expropriate land ownership in order to use it for social justice. With a very high percentage of ownership of land in capitalist countries, with sometimes over 50 percent of the population owning condominiums or townhouses, such a revolution is even less likely today than it was over 150 years ago with much lower property values. The abolition of private property has always remained an illusion because it touches on the basic human need for prosperity. More realistic would be a progressive tax, where the rich pay more than the poor. But even in those countries that strive most strongly for social equalization, such as Scandinavia, this has always been very restrained. And state monopolistic centralization of production, transportation, agribusiness, and many other aspects of economic life has clearly demonstrated through all the attempts of socialist countries that even with radical redistribution and state ownership, new power elites emerge that quickly override previously won civil liberties. Today, it seems less radical but necessary to do more to siphon off the indecently high individual fortunes of the super-rich and return them to the public domain.

For a More Equitable Tax Model

When it comes to the costs of sustainability, a simple logic takes hold: Even companies that have made enormous profits over a long period of time should not be overburdened because jobs depend on them. It should always seem fairer that everyone pays according to the share of the historically given tax burden. The USA boasts of keeping taxes low, especially for the rich. In Germany, taxes start at 28 percent of income for very low earners and end at 44 percent for higher earners, which is a linear model that puts high earners in a much better position than low earners. In this way, high earners in particular benefit across the board. In addition, income from shares or company transfers is often taxed at a lower rate, which makes profits from speculation and branched company constructions particularly attractive. The model is configured in such a way that it inevitably leads to a widening gap between rich and poor. All rich countries follow more or less this path. Neither greater social justice nor the promotion of a sustainable way of life is fundamentally provided for as a target perspective. When politicians promise social justice against the background of this model and do not present a new model, they are deceiving the public. They perpetuate a completely unjust starting position! Look at the tax rates in your country, and you will find out how much fairness there is.

Relieve the Poorer People

The socially unsolved problems all return to sustainability, and the situation for poorer people worsens as costs rise. Taxes can provide incentives, for example, for renewable energies or against high CO_2 emissions. But that is not enough. In sustainability, a tax system would have to emerge that does not predominantly burden the poorer or average income strata with the majority of the costs because they could then more easily refuse to change in the face of constantly rising prices for sustainability. To finance sustainability, a tax progression is needed that still leaves the rich with sufficient incentive to make gains but at the same time narrows the current gap between rich and poor. A tax system that constantly promotes only profit maximization through too low taxation and the numerous opportunities for tax evasion and avoidance for high incomes must be replaced by a system that is fairer and more equitable. Profits from production should be taxed less than profits from speculation in order to promote jobs. At the same time, sustainability should be specially rewarded and reinvestment in sustainability should be encouraged as a profit strategy. There could also be a tax-free basic income tied to an ecologically sound basket of goods. If society fails to achieve a fair distribution of the burdens of sustainability through a more equitable tax system, it will very quickly fail or be driven into lazy compromises. To stay in the simple scheme: The enemies of sustainability and social justice are simply richer, more powerful, more politically assertive.

Higher Taxation of the Rich

The gap between rich and poor can be measured to scale. If a boss earns ten times as much, this may still be understandable if the effort was ten times as much to reach the position. But with an income of 100 or 1,000 times, it is hard to imagine that the effort still serves as a yardstick. If everyone then pays according to tax rates that do not increase upward in the same way as inflated incomes, the gap between rich and poor will continue to widen as a result of the system. The more the prices for sustainability rise, the more relevant becomes the question of the fundamental taxation of the rich. The difference between rich and poor has grown unfairly, and the wealth of very few people has become unimaginably large. This does not mean that all the rich should be expropriated but that we need to restore a reasoned measure of profit expectation to the markets to curb the excessive greed of the present. Investments should be worthwhile, but the neoliberal earmarking of all profits has led us into an increasingly strong and, in the long run, extremely problematic social division. The burdens of sustainability are a great social opportunity to counteract this and restore a sense of social fairness to the majority. It is necessary to strive for a high degree of social intelligence on the part of all agents, both nationally and globally, in order to find fair solutions. After all, how can thinking in terms of sustainability and the common good begin if greed is not immediately taxed at last and thereby moderated?

Higher Rewards for Sustainability

Initiatives for sustainable production, fair trade, and sustainable consumption, on the other hand, should receive tax relief in order to provide sufficient incentives for such goods production and consumption. This can and must flank pricing in order not to make consumer goods more expensive than necessary, the distribution of which is desirable in the sense of an ecological transformation.

Notes

1 See, e.g., from the variety of literature on this subject Bilandzic, H. & Sukalla, F. (2019): The Role of Fictional Film Exposure and Narrative Engagement for Personal Norms, Guilt and Intentions to Protect the Climate. *Environmental Communication*, 13(8), 1069–1086; Dasilva, C. (2019): Imagining Decline or Sustainability: Hope, Fear, and Ideological Discourse in Hollywood Speculative Fiction. *Elementa Science of the Anthropocene, Art*, 7, 1–8.
2 See, e.g., Antonides, G. (Ed.) (2017): *Sustainable Consumer Behavior*. Basel u. a.: MDPI.
3 Gardner, G. T. & Stern, P. C. (2002): *Environmental Problems and Human Behavior*. Boston: Pearson Custom Publishing.
4 See, e.g., Kasser, T. (2009): Values and Ecological Sustainability. In: S. R. Kellert & J. G. Speth (Eds.): *The Coming Transformation: Values to Sustain Human and Natural Communities* (180–204). New Haven: Yale School of Forestry and Environment; Kasser, T. (2011): Cultural Values and the Well-Being of Future Generations: A Cross-National Study. *Journal of Cross-Cultural Psychology*, 42(2), 206–215.
5 As a classical approch to understand the attitude-behavior-gap see, e.g., Fishbein, M. & Ajzen, I. (1975): *Belief, Attitude, Intention and Behavior*. Reading, MA; see also as an easy introduction. https://hbr.org/2019/07/the-elusive-green-consumer
6 Cf., e.g., Chang, C.–H., Kidman, G., & Wi, A. (Eds.) (2020): *Issues in Teaching and Learning of Education for Sustainability: Theory into Practice*. London and New York: Routledge; Cook, J. W. (Ed.) (2019): *Sustainability, Human Well-Being, and the Future of Education*. Cham: Palgrave Macmillan/Springer Nature Switzerland.
7 Even learning from disasters is difficult, cf. the classic text Slovic, P. (1987): Perception of Risk. *Science*, 236, 280–284; with regard to case analyses, e.g., Kamiya, S. & Yanase, N. (2019): Learning from Extreme Catastrophes. *Journal of Risk and Uncertainty*, 59, 85–124; Meyer, R. J. (2012): Failing to Learn from Experience about Catastrophes: The Case of Hurricane Preparedness. *Journal of Risk and Uncertainty*, 45, 25–50; Rheinberger, C. M. & Treich, N. (2017): Attitudes Toward Catastrophe. *Environmental & Resource Economics*, 67(3, 10), 609–636.
8 There is extensive psychological research that helps to confirm this. See as introductions, e.g., Clayton, S. & Manning, C. (Eds.) (2018): *Psychology and Climate Change*. London: Academic Press; Clayton, S., Manning, C. M., & Hodge, C. (2014): *Beyond Storms & Droughts: The Psychological*

Impacts of Climate Change. Washington, DC: American Psychological Association and ecoAmerica; Clayton, S., Devine-Wright, P., Stern, P. C., Whitmarsh, L., Carrico, A., Steg, L., Swim, J., & Bonnes, M. (2015): Psychological Research and Global Climate Change. *Nature Climate Change*, 5, 640–646.

9 For example, Stevenson, K. & Peterson, N. (2015): Motivating Action through Fostering Climate Change Hope and Concern and Avoiding Despair among Adolescents.*Sustainability, MDPI, Open Access Journal*, 8(1), 1–10.

10 See, e.g., Luetz, J. M., Margus, R. & Prickett, B. (2020): Human Behavior Change for Sustainable Development. Perspectives Informed by Psychology and Neuroscience. In: Leal Filho, W. et al. (Hg.): *Quality Education, Encyclopedia of the UN Sustainable Development Goals*. Cham: Springer Nature.

11 See, with some examples, Meireis, T. & Rippl, G. (Hg.) (2019): *Cultural Sustainability. Perspectives from the Humanities and Social Sciences.* London and New York: Routledge.

12 See as a classical text Adams, J. (1995): *Risk*. London, UK: Routledge, Taylor & Francis Group; Posner, R. A. (2004): *Catastrophe: Risk and Response*. New York; Oxford University Press.

13 Cf, e.g., Rudel, T. K. (2019): *Shocks, States, and Sustainability: The Origins of Radical Environmental Reforms*. Oxford: Oxford University Press.

14 As one example among many others, Krogman, N. T. & Bergstrom, A. (2018): Sustainable Higher Education Teaching Approaches. In: Dhiman, S. & Marques, J. (Hg.): *Handbook of Engaged Sustainability*. Springer International Publishing.

15 Rather rarely or in limited insights, the world comes into our awareness with a prediction of the crisis in sustainability; see, e.g., Mayer, S., et al. (2014): *The Anticipation of Catastrophe Environmental Risk in North American Literature and Culture*. Heidelberg: Winter.

16 Examples are given in Robertson, M. (2017): *Sustainability Principles and Practice*. London: Routledge.

17 See with a lot of examples Stern, P. C. (2000): Toward a Coherent Theory of Environmentally Significant Behavior. *Journal of Social Issues*, 56, 407–424; Stern, P. C. (2011): Contributions of Psychology to Limiting Climate Change. *American Psychologist*, 66(4), 303–314; Swim, J., Clayton, S., Doherty, T., Gifford, R., Howard, G., Reser, J., Stern, P., & Weber, E. (2011): Psychological Contributions to Understanding and Addressing Global Climate Change: Special Issue. *American Psychologist*, 66(4), 241–328.

18 For example, https://www.theminimalists.com/minimalism/

19 See, e.g., Johnson, B. (2013): *Zero Waste Home. The Ultimate Guide to Simplifying Your Life by Reducing Your Waste*. New York: Scribner.

20 Cf., e.g., Semenza, C., Hall, D. E., Wilson, D. J., Bontempo, B. D., Sailor, D. J., & George, L. A. (2008): Public Perception of Climate Change: Voluntary Mitigation and Barriers to Behavior Change. *American Journal of Preventive Medicine*, 35(5), 479–487.

21 See especially Kahneman, D. (2011): *Thinking, Fast and Slow*. New York: Farrar, Strauss & Giroux; for nudging cf. Thaler, R. & Sunstein, C. R. (2009): *Nudge. Improving Decisions About Health, Wealth, and Happiness*. New York: Penguin.

22 Cf. Sunstein, C. R. (2017): *Human Agency and Behavioral Economics.* Cham: Palgrave Macmillan; Thaler, R. H. (2015): *Misbehaving: The Making of Behavioral Economics.* New York: Norton.

23 With some examples, see https://www.learnz.org.nz/redvale181/bg-standard-f/the-5-r%27s-of-waste-management

24 In the USA, there is a city plan to implement zero waste. But the critical question remains whether this plan is ambitious enough and how it will be implemented. https://www.epa.gov/transforming-waste-tool/how-communities-have-defined-zero-waste. All countries need such plans, but common agreements would also have to be reached globally.

25 An easy introduction can be found, e.g., here: https://www.nature.com/articles/d41586-021-01143-3

26 For energy and food cf., e.g., Haber, W. (2007): Energy, Food, and Land. The Ecological Traps of Humankind. *Environmental Science and Pollution Research,* 14(6), 359–365; for land, see, e.g., Frederiksen, P. & Kristensen, P. (2008): An indicators framework for analysing sustainability impacts of land use change In: Helming, K. Tabbush, P. & Perez-Soba, M. (Eds.): *Sustainability Impact Assessment of Land Use Changes.* Springer, 293–304.

27 Cf. as an introduction, e.g., Millter, T. (2018): *Greenwashing Culture.* New York and London: Routledge; Bowen, F. (2014): *After Greewashing. Symbolic Corporate Environmentalism and Society (Organizations and the Natural Environment).* Cambridge: Cambridge University Press.

28 A short introduction can be found here: https://ethical.net/ethical/what-is-sustainable-housing-materials-designs-systems/. There are a lot of suggestions in the internet already.

29 Emperical data in a Swedish study show among many other examples that the negative carbon effects correlate strongly with existing obesity, smoking, and low education. https://www.nature.com/articles/s41598-019-56924-8

30 An introduction can be found here: https://www.bbc.com/news/science-environment-49238749

31 What a switch to shared traffic might mean is discussed here: Tikoudis, I., et al. (2021), "Exploring the Impact of Shared Mobility Services on CO_2", OECD Environment Working Papers, No. 175, OECD Publishing, Paris. https://doi.org/10.1787/9d20da6c-en

32 Some arguments against e-mobility are discussed here: https://www.dw.com/en/how-eco-friendly-are-electric-cars/a-19441437

33 See, e.g., Spangenberg, J. H. (Hg.) (2019): *Scenarios and Indicators for Sustainable Development. Towards A Critical Assessment of Achievements and Challenges.* Basel u. a.: MDPI.

34 Liverani, A. (2009): Climate Change and Individual Behavior: Considerations for Policy. Policy Research Working Paper 5058. The World Bank Development Economics, Office of the Senior Vice President and Chief Economist, September 2009.

35 See, e.g., Stevenson, R. B., Brody, M., Dillon, J., & Wals, A. E. J. (Eds.) (2013): *International Handbook of Research on Environmental Education.* New York, NY: Routledge; Wilson, L. A. & Stevenson, C. N. (2019): *Building Sustainability Through Environmental Education.* Hershey, PA: IGI Global; Dhiman, S. & Marques, J. (Eds.) (2018): *Handbook of Engaged Sustainability.* Springer International Publishing. https://link.springer.com/referencework/10.1007%2F978-3-319-71312-0; HESI (2020): *Higher*

Education Sustainability Initiative (HESI. https://sustainabledevelopment.un.org/sdinaction/hesi; Scott, W. (2014): Education for Sustainable Development (ESD): A Critical Review of Concept, Potential and Risk. http://dx.doi.org/10.1007/978-3-319-09549-3; see also endnote 124.

36 See, e.g., Angus, I. (2016): *Facing the Anthropocene. Fossil Capitalism and the Crisis of the Earth System.* New York: Monthly Review Press; Dryzek, J. S., Norgaard, R. B., & Schlosberg, D. (Eds.) (2011): *The Oxford Handbook of Climate Change and Society.* New York: Oxford University Press; Grin, J., Rotman, J., Schot, J. (Eds.) (2010): *Transitions to Sustainable Development: New Directions in the Study of Long Term Transformative Change.* New York and London: Routledge.

37 Even if many may not share the anti-capitalist path, quite a few arguments from this spectrum cannot be dismissed out of hand; see, e.g., Altvater, E. (2016): The Capitalocene, or, Geoengineering Against Capitalism's Planetary Boundaries. In: Moore, J. W. (Ed.): *Anthropocene or Capitalocene? Nature, History, and the Crisis of Capitalism.* Oakland, CA: PM Press, 138–152; Haraway, D. (2015): Anthropocene, Capitalocene, Plantationocene, Chthulucene. Making Kin. *Environmental Humanities*, 6, 159–165; Haraway, D. (2016): *Staying With the Trouble: Making Kin in the Chthulucene.* Durham, NC: Duke University Press.

38 See, e.g., Bryant, R. L. (Hg.) (2015): *The International Handbook of Political Ecology.* Cheltenham, UK: Edward Elgar; Peet, R., Robbins, P., & Watts, M. J. (Eds.) (2011): *Global Political Ecology.* London: Routledge; Perreault, T., Bridge, G., & McCarthy, J. (Hg.) (2015): *The Routledge Handbook of Political Ecology.* London: Routledge; Swyngedouw, E. & Wilson, J. (Eds.) (2014): *The Post-Political and Its Discontents.* Edinburgh: Edinburgh University Press.

39 See, e.g., Norberg, J. (2016): *Progress. Ten Reasons to Look Forward to the Future.* London: Oneworld Publications.

40 Like Rosling, H., Rosling Rönnlund, A., & Rosling, O. (2018): *Factfulness. Ten Reasons We're Wrong About the World-And Why Things Are Better Than You Think.* New York: Flatiron Books.

41 Pinker, S. (2018): *Enlightenment Now: The Case for Reason, Science, Humanism and Progress.* London: Allen Lane.

42 The change in education in more recent times is reflected, for example, by Kalantzis, M. & Cope, B. (2008): *New Learning: Elements of a Science of Education.* Cambridge: Cambridge University Press. Earlier on John Dewey had already provided an important basis for describing the necessary change in learning, as discussed in part III, endnote 47.

43 Cf. endnote 42.

44 What is considered successful in today's learning validates the Deweyan Way. It corresponds to a pragmatist and constructivist theory of learning. See, e.g., Hattie, J. (2009): *Visible Learning. A Synthesis of Over 800 Meta-Analyses Relating to Achievement.* London and New York: Routledge; Hattie, J. (2012): *Visible Learning for Teachers: Maximizing Impact on Learning.* London and New York: Routledge.

45 See from the many researches, e.g., Nielsen, K. S., Clayton, S., Stern, P. C., Dietz, T., Capstick, S., & Whitmarsh, L. (2020): How Psychology Can Help Limit Climate Change. *American Psychologist.* Online First Publication, March 23, 2020; Ulluwishewa, R. (2018): Education in

Human Values. Planting the Seed of Sustainability in Young Minds. In: Dhiman, S. & Marques, J. (Eds.): *Handbook of Engaged Sustainability*. Springer International Publishing.

46 Cf. part II., endnote 52.

47 Especially health is deeply connected to questions of sustainability, see, e.g., Ebi, K. L., Frumkin, H., & Hess, J. J. (2017): Protecting and Promoting Population Health in the Context of Climate and Other Global Environmental Changes. *Anthropocene*, 19, 1–12; the barriers to behavior change are similar to those in sustainability, see, e.g., Kelly, M. P. & Barker, M. (2016): Why Is Changing Health-Related Behaviour so Difficult? *Public Health*, 136, 109–116; Wood, W. & Quinn, J. M. (2005): Habits and the Structure of Motivation in Everyday Life. In: Forgas, J. P., Williams, K. D., & Hippel, W. (Hg.) (2005): *Social Motivation: Conscious and Unconscious Processes*. New York: Cambridge University Press, 55–70.

48 Chabay, I. (2020): Vision, Identity, and Collective Behavior Change on Pathways to Sustainable Futures. *Evolutionary and Institutional Economics Review*, 17, 153.

49 Cf., e.g., Ison, R. & Straw, E. (2020): *The Hidden Power of Systems Thinking: Governance in a Climate Emergency*. London and New York: Routledge.

50 See, e.g., Beatty, A. (2012): *Climate Change Education*. Washington, DC: The National Academies Press; Chang, C.-H. (2014): *Climate Change Education: Knowing, Doing and Being*. London and New York: Routledge; Palmer, J. (1998): *Environmental Education in the 21st Century: Theory, Practice, Progress and Promise*. London and England: Routledge.

51 Cf., e.g., Strachan, G. (2012): Wwf Professional Development Framework of Teacher Competences for Learning for Sustainability. Woking: WWF-UK, 6.

52 The social issue must be at the forefront when it comes to the cost of sustainability. See, e.g., Gore, T. (2015): Extreme Carbon Inequality: Why the Paris Climate Deal Must Put the Poorest, Lowest Emitting and Most Vulnerable People First. Oxfam International. https://policy-practice. oxfam.org/resources/extreme-carbon-inequality-why-the-paris-climate-deal-must-put-the-poorest-lowes-582545/

53 Cf., e.g., Salomon, E., Preston, J. L., & Tannenbaum, M. B. (2017): Climate Change Helplessness and the (De)moralization of Individual Energy Behavior. *Journal of Experimental Psychology: Applied*, 23(1), 15–28.

54 The pricimg must always be combined with behavioral changes; see, e.g., Malyan, R. S. & Duhan, P. (Hg.) (2019): *Green Consumerism. Perspectives, Sustainability, and Behavior*. Toronto and New Jersey: Apple Academic Press.

55 See, e.g., part I., endnote 56; part II., endnote 49.

4 Outrage, Resist, Demand

In 2010, Stéphan Hessel explained why it is time to be outraged and to dare to resist. When he calls out to us in his little pamphlet "Time for Outrage!" that we must defend ourselves against a greedy, inhuman capitalism that does not sufficiently respect human rights, that is selfish and destroys the environment, and that only proclaims freedom and equality as an empty shell, he hits the nerve of our time.

Sustainable, Outrage!

Sustainability is today practically seen, despite the Green Movement, as the ideal of a still too small group of friends, which is aspired to, but not a fact to which we can safely refer just because more than in the past is spoken and written about it. The empty promises regarding sustainability, Fridays for Future correctly conclude, must be overcome; it is outrageous how today humanity is deceived and deceives itself every day! Those who fight against the empty promises find themselves facing a majority of governments that rather offer people a still somehow survivable imbalance between economy and ecology. In this imbalance, at least the richer people of the richer countries could still maintain their chances of survival longer than others with the maximum possible satisfaction of their needs. Survival is more difficult for the poorer because they lack the resources to make provisions. All in all, however, all those who manage to survive will say in the future that the best times were in the past.

Only joint, global action, a prioritization of sustainable approaches, will help to overcome the position of waiting and insisting on one's own advantages. Make it clear to everyone that the supposed advantages of postponed sustainable actions mean disadvantages for everyone in the long run!

DOI: 10.4324/9781003276449-4

Join Movements, Form Your Own!

Fridays for Future is a movement that makes clear, concise, and tar-
geted demands. They demand compliance with the goals of the Paris
Climate Agreement and thus the 1.5-degree target. Nationally, they
are demanding that all countries phase out fossil energies faster than
governments want. They are not making radical demands; they give
necessary and realistic insights justified by the sciences – short-term
goals. Over 27,000 scientists support this (https://www.scientists4fu-
ture.org/). Even if some groups like Extinction Rebellion, Greenpeace,
and others partly demand even faster or stricter measures, the current
policy shows that it still does not trust science far enough and over-
estimates its own opinion and economic interests. But there is only a
limited window of opportunity left for reversal.

Given the urgency of change, it makes little sense for the sustainable to argue about individual aspects of sustainability and lose sight
of the real opponents. We absolutely must overcome the disunity
within the sustainability movements! The commonalities between the
different agents should be emphasized immediately, also with regard
to the different scope and radicality of their programs! But at the same
time, the radicality of the necessary change must not be sacrificed
again to the interests of certain groups. The economy and the selective
interest of those who benefit from the existing unsustainability will
resist change as long as they are not forced to face new majorities.

**Sustainable ones, get outraged and form new
majorities! To this end, gather together, discuss your
actions at any time and in any place: Act and fight
for sustainability to give humanity a future!**

All of us sustainable people are united by one common goal:
We want to save our planet! We are many, hundreds, thousands,
millions, and we are serious! May all the greedy, thoughtless, and
selfish back away from us, may they recognize our courage and
determination! Humanity today is on the verge of losing everything – but there is still hope; there is still "a world to win"!
Sustainables of the world, unite!

Index

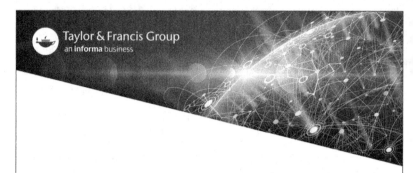

Printed in the United States
by Baker & Taylor Publisher Services